Many can't forgive. Some won't forg[...] [r]eality,
too few Christians know how to pr[...] [re]gard,
Authentic Forgiveness is indeed a vi[...] [J]ohn
has written this book. It is written [...] of a
pastor, and the insightfulness of a c[...] [ex]egete. It is a highly
commendable read!

Rev Edmund Chan
Leadership Mentor, Covenant Evangelical Free Church, Singapore
Founder, Global Alliance of Intentional Disciple Making Churches

Forgiveness is easy – until you meet real people! John Tran has given us the
gift of a theologically articulate and practical resource for helping people in a
local congregation to forgive each other and engage more deeply in community.
"Forgiveness is costly," Tran writes, "and we desperately need it." Whenever
people gather together, hurt, offense, and violence are often realities that must
be dealt with. As Christ followers, we cannot avoid these realities but must
work through these challenges and practice authentic forgiveness in our faith
communities. Tran guides us on that path – biblically and practically.

Kurt Fredrickson, PhD
Associate Dean, Doctor of Ministry Program,
Associate Professor of Pastoral Ministry,
Fuller Theological Seminary, Pasadena, California, USA

Authentic forgiveness requires not only a thoroughly biblical and theological
understanding as its foundation but also a practical strategy addressing the
milieu of local church ministries with realistic cultural constraint. This book
combines the best of both worlds, offering an inspiring paradigm for action
among pastoral colleagues in urban Asian contexts and beyond.

Rev Stephen Lee, PhD
President and Lam Ko Kit Tak Professor of Biblical Studies,
China Graduate School of Theology, Hong Kong

Authentic Forgiveness is a life-transforming book. It explores how human hurts
and conflicts can be deeply and lovingly resolved by courageous acts of Christian
forgiveness. It calls upon readers to examine their own cultural blind spots –
whether these be Chinese habits of condoning sin in the name of harmony or
Western individualistic thinking which understands forgiveness as a private act

of intrapsychic release. It challenges many popular notions of forgiveness which either cheapen grace or distort Christian forgiveness. Authentic forgiveness, as John Tran persuasively argues, must consist of forgiveness, repentance, and reconciliation. Forgiveness can only come to consummation when there is genuine repentance on the part of the offender and reconciliation between the injured person and the offender. Tran invites readers to step out of their comfort zones to deal with past hurts so as to experience the wonderful joy of mended relationships when forgiveness is practiced in an authentic and biblical way. This is a must-read for pastors and Christians who truly want to follow Christ in this world of broken relationships.

Maureen Yeung Marshall, PhD
Professor Emerita of Biblical Studies,
Former President,
Evangel Seminary, Hong Kong

In proposing a strategy to implement the biblical vision of forgiveness in a local context, this book situates itself at the intersection of theological, cultural, and ecclesial concerns and practices. Through the lens of a wider redemptive-historical framework embedded in the biblical text, it provides a strong and effective critique of both the "eastern" prioritization of social harmony and the "western" preoccupation with self-healing. The particularity of its context allows for a wider application in a time when Christian communities are increasingly finding themselves blessed by culturally diverse groups of believers. As such, this book deserves a place on the shelves of conscientious pastors and Christian leaders.

David W. Pao, PhD
Professor of New Testament,
Chair, New Testament Department,
Trinity Evangelical Divinity School, Deerfield, Illinois, USA

Global Perspectives Series

Authentic Forgiveness

Langham
GLOBAL LIBRARY

Authentic Forgiveness

A Biblical Approach

John C. W. Tran

Langham

GLOBAL LIBRARY

© 2020 John C. W. Tran

Published 2020 by Langham Global Library
An imprint of Langham Publishing
www.langhampublishing.org

Langham Publishing and its imprints are a ministry of Langham Partnership

Langham Partnership
PO Box 296, Carlisle, Cumbria, CA3 9WZ, UK
www.langham.org

ISBNs:
978-1-78368-773-2 Print
978-1-78368-774-9 ePub
978-1-78368-775-6 Mobi
978-1-78368-776-3 PDF

John C. W. Tran has asserted his right under the Copyright, Designs and Patents Act, 1988 to be identified as the Author of this work.

All rights reserved. No part of this publication may be reproduced, stored in a retrieval system or transmitted, in any form or by any means, electronic, mechanical, photocopying, recording or otherwise, without the prior written permission of the publisher or the Copyright Licensing Agency.

Requests to reuse content from Langham Publishing are processed through PLSclear. Please visit www.plsclear.com to complete your request.

All Scripture quotations, unless otherwise indicated, are taken from the Holy Bible, New International Version®, NIV®. Copyright ©1973, 1978, 1984, 2011 by Biblica, Inc.™ Used by permission of Zondervan.

All names used in the stories in this book have been changed to protect the confidentiality of those involved.

British Library Cataloguing-in-Publication Data
A catalogue record for this book is available from the British Library

ISBN: 978-1-78368-773-2

Cover & Book Design: projectluz.com

Langham Partnership actively supports theological dialogue and an author's right to publish but does not necessarily endorse the views and opinions set forth here or in works referenced within this publication, nor can we guarantee technical and grammatical correctness. Langham Partnership does not accept any responsibility or liability to persons or property as a consequence of the reading, use or interpretation of its published content.

To my beloved wife, Angela, for her love and care over the past thirty years, for patiently supporting me to pursue what God has placed on my heart.

To my wonderful children, Joshua and Rachel, for their prayers, support, and understanding, and the joy they bring to me.

To my other family members, who always love and encourage me.

To those who are broken and hurt.

To our God who cares.

CONTENTS

Foreword

Forgiving Is Hard Work – It Is *Heart* Work, Not Just *Head* Work

Sue Monk Kidd, in her wonderful novel, *The Secret Life of Bees*, writes about a young girl who has been spiritually, physically, and psychologically abused. Out of her pain, Lily expresses incisive wisdom about many things, especially about the difficulty of forgiving: "People in general, would rather die than forgive. It's *that* hard. If God said in plain language, 'I'm giving you a choice, forgive or die,' a lot of people would go ahead and order their coffin."[1]

Forgiving is so difficult for many of us that we create a wide range of substitute solutions that allow us to pretend we are being good about it all or too mature to be troubled by another's action, but it is all a strategy for saving face – our own face in particular.

John Tran asks hard questions. John Tran does not settle for easy answers. John Tran has invited us to walk this hard path with him because it is the path to authentic, not imitation, forgiveness. Read on, and you will be challenged and stimulated and provoked to rethink and reconsider what forgiving and being forgiven are all about.

Speaking from the world of Chinese Christian faith, Tran discusses the primary model of forgiving in Chinese culture and relationships, which is that of the father forgiving the prodigal son (in appropriate top-down filial order). But what about the son who longs to forgive the prodigal father? (Is this filial piety or recognition of tragic failure and the need for grace?) Is the ultimate model of authentic forgiveness that of Stephen forgiving his stoners? (Acts 7:60). Or of Jesus praying for his executioners? (Luke 23:34). Or are these the ultimate example – indeed the soul – of enemy love given in mercy where there is no repentance and authentic forgiving is impossible?

---

1. Sue Monk Kidd, *The Secret Life of Bees* (2002), 277.

Is authentic forgiving, if we take love and mercy and justice seriously in our understanding of it, more like the moment when Jesus sets free the taxman Zacchaeus from his life of corruption as he pledges restitution and a new life of justice in community? (Luke 19:6–10). That would follow what Jesus has just taught (Luke 17:3–4).

No two cases of injury and forgiveness are truly alike. Each experience of pain and the struggle to regain balance, healing, grace, and inner peace is unique; each journey toward reconciliation and reopening of the future follows its own course. This book does not hesitate to take on this hard work of urging and guiding readers to love and seek reconciliation.

In the authentic forgiveness portrayed here, the injured person will feel the injury, feel the pain, and clearly see the injury for what it is. But the sufferer will also see the other as human, and indeed recover the other's co-humanity. No matter the nature or extent of the wrongdoing, the one who forgives will restore perceptions of the offender's worth and value the other in spite of the wrong done.

But authentic forgiveness is not just this change in how you see the offender, and if you try "to forgive and forget" at this point, it is a matter of the head and not the heart, an act of will but not the soul. We need time to sort it out, to get in touch with the heart, to withdraw and reflect until head and heart come together in a desire to relate again.

Tran's work recognizes how hard it is to face intolerable and unacceptable hurt in the heart and soul, to sort out the anger, to make room for the sadness, and to realize that, despite the injury done, the other is equally precious. Tran shows how important it is to cultivate an attitude of love for the offender.

Authentic Forgiveness points us towards the search for true reconciliation, where people risk communication, extend trust, and work through the anger and pain. In such reconciliation, genuine intentions and authentic repentance reopen the future to live in moral community.

Authentic Forgiveness is a book that will enrich your life with its wise counsel on how to work at living in the midst of tough situations by daily returning to care about justice and trust and faithfulness in deepening loving relationships.

David Augsburger, PhD
Professor of Pastoral Care and Counseling,
Fuller Theological Seminary, Pasadena, California, USA

Acknowledgments

I would like to express my heartfelt gratitude to Dr David Augsburger, my teacher and mentor, for inspiring me to discover the importance of biblically based forgiveness, encouraging me to write this book, and giving me his invaluable and continual support throughout the past years. Without him, I could not have come this far.

I also thank the many good friends and colleagues in my church, former classmates, pastors of other churches, and professors at China Graduate School of Theology in Hong Kong and at Fuller Theological Seminary for the precious advice given as I completed this work.

Abstract

Can anyone escape conflict, hurt, and pain? How best can we deal with these unwelcome and difficult realities?

In life, conflict and hurt are inevitable. The only way to avoid them altogether is to refuse to enter into relationships. The failure to respond appropriately to conflict is destructive to life. The best way to transform conflict and hurt from being life-destructive to being life-constructive is to forgive and to be forgiven. Authentic, biblically based forgiveness is a gift that God offers to humanity so that hurt can be healed, the cycle of retaliation broken, a painful past healed, and estranged relationships reconciled and restored.

What exactly is biblically based forgiveness?

Forgiveness has a variety of meanings and expressions within different cultures. Not all these kinds of forgiveness are biblically based; nor are they equally life-transforming. Because of such cultural influences, many Christians – who are rooted in Chinese tradition or influenced by Western individualistic cultures – perceive and practice forgiveness in a way that deviates from and trivializes biblically based forgiveness. For example, some forgive in order to avoid conflict and maintain harmony but in a way that ignores truth and justice. Others forgive in order to achieve self-healing but ignore reconciliation of the broken relationship. Some forgive by forgetting the past in an attempt to escape from reality, but they can hardly forget the pain.

This book defines "authentic forgiveness" as forgiveness that is biblically based and free from distortions caused by cultural influences. Authentic forgiveness offered by the victim is consummated when there is genuine repentance by the offender and reconciliation of broken relationship between the parties involved.

The purpose of this book is to inspire and motivate Christians to identify what authentic forgiveness truly is and to confront the human tendency to trivialize it due to cultural influences. Trivialization makes forgiveness an easy path, but it reduces the transforming power of authentic forgiveness. Further, the book sets out concrete steps that may be followed in order to practice authentic forgiveness and receive the blessings that God intends through this process. The closing chapters describe a one-year plan for churches that want to help their members to identify and practice authentic forgiveness.

May those who are broken and in deep pain be healed and released from bondage!

1

Location, Location, Location: Forgiving in a Chinese Context

Sharon's Story[1]

A few years ago, a pastor related how his wife, Sharon, had been molested repeatedly by her brother when she was a child. When Sharon grew up, she shared her experience with a counseling and prayer team, and sought their help. The counseling and prayer team "taught" her to forgive her brother unconditionally, yet without addressing the grave wrong that had been done to her. Sharon willed herself to pray the "forgiveness prayer," but she did so without true feeling and was left wondering how to deal with her hurt and the broken relationship with her brother. One day, she courageously confronted her brother, in the presence of her parents and sisters. However, both her parents and her brother ignored her, saying that all this had happened a long time ago when her brother was still young and that they did not want to disrupt the harmony within the family. They simply told Sharon to forget about it. Her brother did not offer a genuine apology and her parents did not urge him to repent. They sought no justice in the situation.

Sharon had been hurt three times. First, she was hurt by being molested as a child. Second, she was hurt when the counseling and prayer team asked her to forgive unconditionally without helping her to deal with the injustice and the broken relationship, leaving her confused and puzzled about the nature of true forgiveness. Third, she was deeply hurt when her parents ignored both her pain and her request for her brother's repentance. When Sharon was molested, her brother was already a teenager. Was that

---

1. All names mentioned in the stories in this book have been changed to protect the confidentiality of those involved.

really too young to be held responsible? Sharon asked a valid question: "What is true forgiveness?"

Consider the actions of Sharon's parents and the counseling and prayer team in the light of Jesus's words: "If your brother or sister sins against you, rebuke them; and if they repent, forgive them" (Luke 17:3) and "If your brother or sister sins, go and point out their fault . . . If they listen to you, you have won them over" (Matt 18:15). For true forgiveness to take place, Jesus requires pointing out a person's fault, bringing justice to the victim, requesting the offender to repent, encouraging the victim to forgive, and the parties reconciling with one another. What Sharon's parents and the counseling and prayer team did deviates from and trivializes what Jesus teaches us.

True forgiveness is a hard but necessary path!

Conflict, evil, and hurt are inevitable in life. We need to forgive and be forgiven because forgiveness is a transforming process. In his book *Helping People Forgive*, Augsburger explains that this process "allows us to change our minds, begin again, and risk further relationship. . . . This breaking of the cycle of blind retaliation or judicial retribution allows persons, relationships, or institutions to start over, to begin again."[2]

Many people misunderstand what forgiveness truly is. It is not forgetting the past, overlooking wrongdoing, maintaining harmony at all costs, or a one-sided act to release pain. Rather, it is a social transaction that comprises genuine repentance by the offender, the offer of forgiveness by the victim to the offender, and restoration of the broken relationship of the parties involved.[3]

Since it is impossible to avoid conflict, evil, and hurt without removing ourselves from all relationships, it is important to respond proactively and rightly. True, biblically based forgiveness is God's precious gift to humanity; it is able to transform conflict, evil, and hurt from being life-destructive to being life-constructive by healing people's hurt, releasing them from the cycle of retaliation, and empowering them to reconcile. But not all kinds of forgiveness practiced in different traditions and cultures are biblically based or equally life-transforming. In his book *Conflict Mediation across Cultures*, Augsburger points out that forgiveness has many faces in different cultures, as each culture shapes its own understanding and practice of forgiveness based on its central

---

2. David W. Augsburger, *Helping People Forgive* (Louisville, KY: Westminster John Knox, 1996), 9.

3. Augsburger, *Helping People Forgive*, 14–16.

values.[4] Thus, forgiveness that carries different meanings, expressions, and practices in different traditions and cultures deviates – in varying degrees and aspects – from true, biblically based forgiveness. Such deviations trivialize the transforming power of biblically based forgiveness. This kind of trivialization takes place in many churches in Hong Kong and around the world.

For the people of Hong Kong, as well as those in countries with a similar cultural background, their understanding and practice of forgiveness is shaped by the values of their Eastern roots and Western culture. Hong Kong is an international city. A Chinese person raised in Hong Kong is rooted in the Confucianism of thousands of years, while also continually influenced by Western culture. Therefore, the way in which the people of Hong Kong deal with relationships and forgiveness is a mixture of these two cultures. Further, for those who become Christians, these Eastern and Western influences affect their interpretation of the Bible and the way they understand forgiveness. Chinese tradition, rooted in Confucianism, and Western culture distort to varying extents the way many Christians in Hong Kong perceive and practice forgiveness. The Christians of my church, Evangelical Free Church of China Jachin Church of Hong Kong (Jachin Church), are no exception.

Presently, over one thousand people attend Jachin Church, which is among the top fifty churches in Hong Kong in terms of population. I am the founding and senior pastor of Jachin Church. I also serve on the board of directors of China Graduate School of Theology, one of the major seminaries in Asia, and as an executive committee member of the board of directors of the Evangelical Free Church of China in Hong Kong (EFCC). In Hong Kong, EFCC is one of the top three largest denominations in terms of population and there are around 60 churches belonging to the denomination of EFCC.

My own experiences in ministry, and my discussions with numerous pastors and professors, indicate that a great many Christians perceive and practice forgiveness in a distorted manner. Such distortions arise mainly due to their understanding of forgiveness being tainted, in varying degrees, by Chinese tradition rooted in Confucianism and Western culture. For example, some forgive by forgetting the past and focusing on the future; some forgive by passive acceptance; others forgive in order to avoid conflict and maintain harmony; still others forgive in order to achieve self-healing, yet without dealing with the damaged relationship; and some forgive by pretending all is well again.

---

4. David W. Augsburger, *Conflict Mediation across Cultures* (Louisville, KY: Westminster John Knox, 1992), 18–27, 262–264.

This is not authentic forgiveness. God not only wants people to unilaterally forgive and be healed, he also wants them to repent and reconcile with one another through a process of true forgiveness that is biblically based so that complete healing can occur and genuine communion can be restored. This book defines "authentic forgiveness" as forgiveness that is biblically based and free from distortions caused by cultural influences. Authentic forgiveness offered by the victim is consummated when there is genuine repentance by the offender and reconciliation of broken relationship between the parties involved. Genuine repentance of the offender should consist of three elements: remorse, restitution, and renewal.[5]

This book aims to inspire and motivate Christians to identify and practice authentic forgiveness and to confront the human tendency to trivialize it due to cultural influences. It includes a one-year plan for churches wishing to help their members to identify and practice authentic forgiveness.

Only through authentic forgiveness can people be released from their broken past and damaged relationships reconciled to the full extent that God originally intended. Biblical examples of authentic forgiveness – encompassing both repentance and reconciliation – are found in the story of Joseph and his brothers, the parable of the prodigal son, and in the exhortations of Leviticus 6:1–7, Matthew 5:23–24 and 18:15–17, and Luke 17:3–4. Where there is a lack of genuine repentance on the part of the offender or the failure of one or both parties to strive for reconciliation of the broken relationship, authentic forgiveness is undermined. Anything less than authentic forgiveness is inadequate for complete healing. For various reasons, it is not always viable to achieve authentic forgiveness – for instance, unrepentance, unwillingness to forgive, or death of a party. In such instances, we are to grieve the failure of full reconciliation as David did when pursued by King Saul (see, for example, David's prayer in Ps 57), and we are to love and pray for our enemies as Jesus commands (Matt 5:44).

Factors That Shape the Christian's Perception of Forgiveness

As noted previously, the way Christians in Hong Kong – and other places with similar cultural backgrounds – perceive relationships and forgiveness is shaped by three factors: Eastern tradition, Western culture, and the Bible. Indeed, even their interpretation of "forgiveness passages" in the Bible is influenced by their Eastern roots and westernized values.

---

5. Augsburger, *Helping People Forgive*, 14–16.

Eastern Tradition

Chinese values and expressions are deeply rooted in Confucianism. Traditional Chinese, rooted in Confucianism, tend to be relatively hierarchical, respectful, harmonious, and less expressive as compared to those brought up in Western countries. These characteristics are discussed briefly here and in greater detail in chapter 2.

Hierarchy and respect

It is customary to pay full respect to seniors. For example, it is usually considered offensive to refer to one's father or mother by name, and children, regardless of age, are obliged to call their parents "father" and "mother"; it is also considered impolite to call a teacher by name without using a title such as Professor, Doctor, Mister, Miss, or Teacher. While respect is a good Chinese tradition, when there is wrongdoing which involves an older person, confession does not come easily. Inquiring into the issues involving the faults of senior persons would cause them to lose face and is considered a lack of respect.[6] Thus, many traditional fathers rarely say, "I am sorry." Issues concerning conflict and hurt between parents and children are seldom discussed due to a need to save face and a desire to show respect.

An elderly Chinese pastor, who is a grandfather himself, shared that whenever he tried to talk to his father about a childhood hurt, his father refused to discuss it. The hurt was not properly dealt with even though the pastor was ready to forgive. Ultimately, his father passed away, leaving the wound untouched. The pastor said that, even though he tried very hard, time did not help him to forget the wound. Without authentic forgiveness, it is difficult to forget the pain of the past.

Less emotionally expressive

Among the older generation, not only do many traditional fathers rarely admit "I am sorry," they seldom say the words "I love you," even to their wives and children. In 2016, at a public seminar held in Hong Kong, a world-famous Chinese theologian shared that he and his sisters had never heard their father – a reputable pastor and professor who had passed away a few years ago – explicitly express his love for them by saying "I love you." It was not that their father did not love them, but he was acting according to culture;

---

6. Augsburger, *Conflict Mediation*, 262–266.

and traditional Chinese rarely express love or emotion verbally and directly; they prefer to do so using other means such as by their actions or in writing.

Harmony

Harmony is a precious core value in Chinese tradition. When facing conflict and hurt, a traditional Chinese may tend to overlook a wrongful act in order to maintain harmony, at least on the surface. But sometimes, this kind of "harmony" is at the expense of justice and fairness.

Thus, lack of expressiveness and the need to safeguard harmony tend to cause many traditional Chinese to avoid facing sensitive issues, to bury these matters and feelings deep in their hearts, and to shy away from holding accountable those responsible. This kind of shallow harmony is not genuine – beneath the undiscussed and unresolved conflicts and hurts, hearts are breaking and relationships are decaying. Sharon's case is a typical example. Authentic forgiveness goes beyond harmony; it involves genuine and in-depth discussion of the conflicts and hurts in order that the offender is given an opportunity to confess and repent, and also to be reconciled with the offended.

Many people in Korea, Taiwan, and mainland China are also deeply rooted in Confucianism. Therefore, the way they see and act with respect to relationships, forgiveness, and community is similar to that of the traditional Chinese people of Hong Kong.

Western Culture

Hong Kong was a British colony for over 150 years and has been an international city opened to the Western world for decades. Over the past few decades, Hong Kong has experienced strong economic growth and is now ranked in the top twenty in GDP per capita in the world.[7] It has developed into a major global trade hub, financial center, and famous tourist city, and was ranked among the top seven in terms of global competitiveness by the World Economic Forum.[8] In this international city, the values of the Chinese people of Hong Kong are – in varying degrees, depending on their age and exposure and openness to

---

7. Statista, "The 20 countries with the largest gross domestic product (GDP) per capita in 2017," accessed 27 May 2019, https://www.statista.com/statistics/270180/countries-with-the-largest-gross-domestic-product-gdp-per-capita/.

8. World Economic Forum, "The Global Competitiveness Report 2018," accessed 27 May 2019, http://reports.weforum.org/global-competitiveness-report-2018/competitiveness-rankings/.

Western culture – products of both the East and the West. The way they deal with relationships and forgiveness is also a mix of these two cultures.

Western culture is permeated by individualism. On the positive side, individualism emphasizes that every human being has dignity and self-worth – as opposed to being a collection of insignificant atoms in the mass of humanity – and encourages responsibility. The flip side is that individualism promotes, as its central value, an individual's self-interest. Individuals act on their own behalf, and the needs of the individual are regarded as more important than the needs of the community.[9]

Authentic forgiveness is never just about a single individual's need or self-healing; it is a social transaction, restoring and reconciling a broken relationship between the offender and the offended. Due to the emphasis on self-care, forgiveness in an individualistic culture has ceased to be an interpersonal bridge and become an intrapersonal process of self-healing that is unrelated to the community. Unfortunately, in Western cultures, unilateral forgiveness has become the norm due to psychological and sociological reasons such as self-love and the understanding of forgiveness as a private act of intrapsychic release.[10]

As a result of the dual cultural influences of Chinese tradition rooted in Confucianism and Western individualism, many people in Hong Kong interpret forgiveness as a mixture of preserving harmony without dealing with the conflict in depth and acting out of internal self-love without reconciliation of the broken relationship. Sharon's counseling and prayer team is an example of this, since they invited her to forgive as an act of internal self-care without addressing the broken relationship.

Today, individualism influences many churches around the globe, including those in Hong Kong, and so the understanding and practice of forgiveness among Christians is distorted. The kind of forgiveness taught at these churches places less emphasis on the restoration of impaired relationships and lays more stress on intrapsychic release. Gregory Jones, in his book *Embodying Forgiveness*, explains that the unilateral act from an individual paradigm trivializes forgiveness.[11] It makes it therapeutically easy, but the result is damaging to the Christian community because there is no sense of restoration of communion and reconciliation of broken relationships. The unilateral act of forgiveness

---

9. David W. Augsburger, email to the author, 8 November 2016.

10. Augsburger, *Helping People Forgive*, 14.

11. L. Gregory Jones, *Embodying Forgiveness: A Theological Analysis* (Grand Rapids, MI: Eerdmans, 1995), xv, 5.

causes the offender to ignore the need for repentance and reconciliation, which are crucial aspects of authentic forgiveness, both theologically and biblically.

Theological and Biblical Foundations of Authentic Forgiveness

People frequently find themselves trapped in cycles of sin, violence, and revenge. Jones writes, "we are now the heirs of histories and habits of sin and evil that make it difficult, if not impossible, to break out of the cycles of violence and counterviolence, of diminishing and being diminished."[12] Worse, human beings may refuse to acknowledge these cycles or admit that these cycles are problematic and demand an urgent response. But God, by his self-giving love, transcends the human tendency to sin and – through the life, death, and resurrection of Jesus Christ – offers humankind a new beginning. When Jesus, vulnerable in his humanity, was oppressed, betrayed, and abandoned, he did not allow himself to be defined by the pain and injustice caused, and, refusing to perpetuate a cycle of sin, revenge, and violence, broke this cycle by his forgiveness. Jesus, who wills forgiveness, earnestly pleads with all sinners to repent and be reconciled to him. Jesus embodies forgiveness as a new way of life and his followers are called to build the habit of forgiveness in their lives.[13] "Those who are forgiven by Jesus are called to embody that forgiven-ness in the new life signified by communion with Jesus and with other disciples."[14] In so doing, they can break cyclical habits and restore communion.

Authentic forgiveness, in both the Hebrew and Christian Scriptures, is an interpersonal transaction of the offender offering genuine repentance and the offended recognizing and accepting that repentance resulting in reconciliation of the broken relationship. Repentance – consisting of remorse, restitution, and renewal – and reconciliation of broken relationships are central to the process of authentic forgiveness. This is illustrated in the story of Joseph and his brothers, the parable of the prodigal son, and in the exhortations of Leviticus 6:1–7, Matthew 5:23–24, 18:15–17, and Luke 17:3–4.

In the story of the prodigal son, the younger son was filled with remorse as he confessed that he had sinned against heaven and against his father. His restitution and renewal came when he felt contrition and asked for nothing but to be a slave to serve his father. Reconciliation occurred when the father, following the son's repentance, welcomed his lost son with full honor. Since

---

12. Jones, *Embodying Forgiveness*, 115.

13. Jones, 110, 115–121.

14. Jones, 121.

authentic forgiveness should comprise both repentance and reconciliation, it is incomplete if there is repentance but no reconciliation. The central motif of biblical forgiveness sees reconciliation as its goal. Augsburger points out, "Authentic forgiveness is that cluster of motivations which seeks to regain the brother and the sister in reconciliation . . . The courage to forgive is an excellency of character, a virtue that enables one to act in restoration of personal relationships, to risk in reconstruction of social networks, to commit oneself to live in moral integrity."[15]

For traditional Chinese Christians in Hong Kong, virtue, morality, harmony, and reconstruction of social networks are the continual pursuit of their daily lives since these are the central values of Chinese tradition rooted in Confucianism. But the pursuit of confession, repentance, and justice is a challenge for them since this may disrupt harmony and cause a loss of face. For westernized Chinese Christians in Hong Kong, on whose minds individualism exerts a controlling grip, the difficulty is to subordinate their feelings to moral integrity and to take risks in the reconstruction of community. Authentic forgiveness, however, is not merely about harmony or self-healing but about "justice, love, mercy, and the uncomfortable behavior we call repentance. Reconciliation must struggle with deeper levels of all these and the complexities of restitution and restoration."[16] This kind of authentic forgiveness, comprising both repentance and reconciliation, is not practiced as often as it should be either in Hong Kong or around the globe in churches with similar cultural backgrounds.

Indeed, many Christians are taught to pray for the ability to let go and be healed when they are hurt, and to pray for God's forgiveness when they wrong others. A few years ago, a well-respected international preacher – a British Chinese, educated and residing in London – preached in Hong Kong. He preached powerfully, and with great love, on the theme of forgiveness. He then invited people who had been hurt to respond to an altar call, but he only asked them to pray for healing and the strength to forgive those who had hurt them. While the message was touching and comforting, and many cried and prayed for God's grace and help, it was a unilateral act that did not address the importance of repentance by the offender and reconciliation of the broken relationship. This unilateral act represents a struggle in one's heart, a love of one's enemy, and a willing heart to forgive. While all these are important, they represent only the first step in authentic forgiveness. Jesus taught us to

---

15. Augsburger, *Helping People Forgive*, 115–116.
16. Augsburger, 115.

do much more: "Therefore, if you are offering your gift at the altar and there remember that your brother or sister has something against you, leave your gift there in front of the altar. First go and be reconciled to them; then come and offer your gift" (Matt 5:23–24).

Authentic forgiveness, offered by victims to their offenders, takes its final step when victims reconnect with those who have hurt them. Authentic forgiveness requires one party to repent and the other party to extend grace to the repentant one with both trust and respect. When there is mutual recognition that both repentance and acceptance are genuine and the broken relationship is reconstructed, authentic forgiveness occurs. The victim discovers that the strange chemistry of reconciliation can heal the wound until nothing remains but the remembered scar with a transformed meaning. Such forgiveness results in a deeper and stronger healing and union than before.[17]

Between 2016 and 2018, I led a small group at Jachin Church, helping and encouraging participants to identify and practice authentic forgiveness. After a year spent helping them to connect with God and to be spiritually and mentally healthy, group members were encouraged to identify and pray for their enemies, and to meet them and attempt to reconcile with them.

Ruby's Story

Ruby was a member of this small group. As a child, she had been molested by her father. Not long after, her father divorced her mother and remarried. Ruby experienced deep pain for many years. After learning about authentic forgiveness she decided to practice it. Accompanied by her husband, she approached her father. She did not lash out at him but, instead, apologized for the ways she had wronged him in the past by her revengeful attitude and actions. Her seventy-year-old father wept. He was deeply remorseful about what he had done to his daughter. He apologized, and asked Ruby to forgive him. She cried. She hugged him. She offered forgiveness.

A few months after this incident, I encouraged Ruby to meet with her father and talk through in detail what had happened in her childhood. During that time, her father told her how hurt he was when he had separated from her mother — he became drunk all the time and fought on the streets. With deep remorse and shame, he wept and apologized again. He felt he was not worthy to have his daughter forgive him. She again affirmed her father of the forgiveness and the reconciliation she was willing to extend to him. She became involved in his life and took care of him. Ruby was reconciled with her father.

---

17. David W. Augsburger, *The New Freedom of Forgiveness* (Chicago, IL: Moody, 2000), 32.

Since early 2019, Ruby's mother, father, and her father's second wife have been attending Jachin Church's elders' cell group on a regular basis. The transforming power of authentic forgiveness brought healing, reconciliation, and new life in Christ for these four people.

The Rest of the Book

When someone who has lived under the teaching of Confucianism and the influence of Western culture accepts Jesus as their Lord and personal Savior, this new faith should change the way they understand and practice forgiveness. Genuine repentance and reconciliation of community are central to the process of authentic forgiveness. The purpose of this book is to inspire and motivate pastors and Christians to identify and practice authentic forgiveness, to confront the tendency to trivialize it under cultural influences, and to take concrete steps leading to the practice of authentic forgiveness.

Chapter 2 discusses how Chinese tradition and Western individualism shape and distort the way people in Hong Kong – including Christians – view conflict, as well as how they perceive and practice relationships and forgiveness.

Chapter 3 examines seven books dealing with topics such as the inevitability of conflict and hurt in human life, the progression of sin, what authentic forgiveness means, and the tendency to trivialize it under the cultural influences of both East and West.

Chapter 4 considers the theological and biblical foundations of authentic forgiveness. It examines the theological concepts of God's will for forgiveness and communion and how Christian forgiveness involves communion with God and with one another. It also explores the biblical foundation of authentic forgiveness, including the relationship between repentance and forgiveness in the Old and New Testaments.

Chapters 5 and 6 focus on a ministry plan for any church interested in helping its members to learn about and practice authentic forgiveness. This includes setting goals, developing strategies, recruiting and training pastors and lay leaders, and incorporating quantitative and qualitative measures to assess the effectiveness of this new ministry initiative.

The final chapter is a summary, concluding with a real-life example of how authentic forgiveness blesses a family when family members forgive one another.

2

Influences That Shape and Distort Perceptions and the Practice of Forgiveness

Andy's Story

Andy, a forty-year-old pastor, sought my advice. He had been in full-time ministry for twenty years and was earmarked as the successor of the senior pastor, who had been in office for thirty years. During the last two years of transition of office from the senior pastor to him, Andy had many new ideas about how to grow the church. When he made these suggestions during staff meetings, however, he was accused of disrupting the harmony of the team and challenging the authority of the senior pastor. Once, when Andy said "I don't agree with you" to the senior pastor during a staff meeting, he was accused of being unsubmissive. To publicly express disagreement was rare among the pastoral team, since this was viewed as "confrontation" and "disharmony." After months of such "disharmony" in the team, the senior pastor urged the board of deacons to ban many of Andy's plans and ideas. Even though the senior pastor had already reached the age of retirement, he decided to delay retirement for another three to five years. Andy was warned that unless he paid more attention to the tradition of the church and the harmony of the team, spoke less, and submitted to the senior pastor's leadership, he would not be appointed as senior pastor. Andy replied that submission was not a problem as long as matters were discussed thoroughly. He continued to discuss matters in detail and attempt to resolve differences, but this was regarded as aggravating the conflict, being disobedient, and disrupting the harmony. Andy was both angry and sad. The board of deacons asked Andy "not to let the sun go down while he was still angry" and "to let go and let God" handle this matter. The board also asked Andy to reconcile with the senior pastor without dealing with the

13

substance of the issue. Andy was confused as to what they meant. He was also hurt that he was not given any opportunity to discuss the new initiatives.

What had happened here? Listening to Andy's story, I realized that the senior pastor was a traditional Chinese, while Andy was a westernized Chinese, educated in the West. The two men came from two different values systems – and this was the main cause for the conflicts.

Two major factors shape the way people in Hong Kong – and in other countries with similar cultural backgrounds – perceive relationship, conflict, and forgiveness: the Eastern tradition, rooted in Confucianism, and the Western individualistic culture. This chapter examines how these two factors taint the way Christians view conflict and how they perceive and practice authentic forgiveness.

Forgiveness in the Chinese Tradition

Confucianism is the key factor that shapes the way people rooted in the Eastern tradition perceive conflict, relationship, and forgiveness. This section explores how people rooted in Confucianism, including traditional Chinese, view personhood, virtues, values, and relationships, which then become the incubating ground for them to perceive and deal with conflicts, resolution, forgiveness, and reconciliation.

In his *Analects*, Confucius said, "In the application of the rites, harmony is to be prized (禮之用，和為貴)."[1] In the ethics of Confucianism, a person is never viewed as an individual but as part of a community. How traditional Chinese, and those people rooted in Confucianism, live and act in a society are linked with many aspects, such as other people's feelings, the consequence when one has a view different from the majority, family hierarchy, and harmonious relationships. Harmony is the goal, both of personal virtue and of human society.[2] Further, traditional Chinese are relatively humble and inexpressive as compared to Westerners. Confucius once said to his students, "The way of a person of virtue is threefold, but I am not equal to it. Virtuous, he is free from anxieties; wise, he is free from perplexities; courageous, he is free from fear

---

1. Cheuk Fei Man and Check Yim Cheng [文灼非和鄭赤琰], 《中國關係學》 [*The Studies of Chinese Relationship*] (Hong Kong: Hong Kong Chinese University Asia Research Centre, 1996), 19.

2. Man and Cheng, 《中國關係學》 [Studies of Chinese Relationship], 16–19.

(君子道者三，我無能焉：仁者不憂，知者不惑，勇者不懼)."[3] What is interesting about this statement is that Confucius, when teaching his students what a person of virtue should be, began by stating that he was not qualified to be one of these. A surprising statement, since Confucius was the founder of the philosophy. But he was exhibiting this virtue of humility.

Due to inexpressiveness and humility, the older generation may rarely express words of love and appreciation to those who are close to them. They may never say "I love you" or "I am proud of you" in public, or even privately, to their children. Rather, they keep silent about their children's abilities and good deeds. Some older parents may show appreciation of the children of other families but not of their own children. In fact, many traditional Chinese may even publicly deny any praise given to their children or grandchildren by others so that the family can appear to be humble. For example, if a neighbor says to the parents that their child is polite or clever, a typical answer would be, "No, no, no. Not at all! No!" This is very different to how Western parents would typically react to a neighbor who says the same thing.

Harmony, humility, and inexpressiveness are common characteristics of many traditional Chinese and those rooted in Confucianism. The core values and virtues of Confucianism shape the mindset of these people in the areas of relationship, expression, dignity, conflict, and forgiveness in both a personal and communal sense. These can be traced back to the "Five Constant Virtues (五常)" and "Three Cardinal Guides (三綱)."

Five Constant Virtues

Of the Five Constant Virtues (五常), Confucius expounded on three virtues: *Ren* (仁, meaning benevolence), *Yi* (義, meaning righteousness), and *Li* (禮, meaning propriety). Mencius, a follower of Confucius, developed one more virtue, that of *Zhi* (智, meaning wisdom). Later, in the first century BCE, other followers developed the fifth virtue, *Xin* (信, meaning trust). Confucius believed that human beings are different from other species due to their potential for moral virtues. This potential and the development of moral character determine our human dignity. In contrast to the Western values of

---

3. 《中國哲學書電子化計劃》 [China Philosophy Book Online Plan], accessed 17 September 2019, https://ctext.org/analects/xian-wen/zh?searchu=%E5%A4%AB%E5%AD%90.

rationality and self-determination, Confucius emphasized moral virtues as the distinguishing characteristic of humanity.[4]

Mencius believed that a human being is born with four seeds of moral virtue: *Ren, Yi, Li,* and *Zhi*. He said, "Heaven is the author of the virtues in me (天生德於予)."[5] These virtues are as real as the four human limbs. Human beings should cultivate and develop these virtues just like they develop their limbs. Although everyone is born with the potential for these virtues, it is necessary to cultivate, develop, make choices, act, and be provided with a suitable environment in order to realize and practice these virtues and become a moral person. To become a moral person with full moral potential, human effort is crucial. Mencius said, "By nature, humans are nearly alike. By practice, they become very different (性相近也，習相遠也)."[6] Among the four virtues, *Ren* (benevolence) is the highest virtue. The word *Ren* (benevolence) is formed by two Chinese words, "two" and "men," and carries a sense of getting along with one another harmoniously and benevolently. If humans are true to themselves and to others, *Ren* (benevolence) would drive them to love others and *Yi* (righteousness) would motivate them to fulfill their moral duties to others. *Ren* and *Yi* are interrelated and work hand in hand to promote social harmony.[7]

Traditional Chinese put in a great deal of effort to develop *Ren* (benevolence) and *Yi* (righteousness) to become moral persons. By practicing *Li* (propriety), *Ren* (benevolence) and *Yi* (righteousness) can be revealed in a person's life. *Li* (propriety) is the way, route, and standard to achieve *Ren* (benevolence) and *Yi* (righteousness). In practicing *Li* (propriety), there are two phases. The first phase is subduing the self (克己). It requires a person to subdue and cultivate self. This is illustrated by what Confucius once said: "Look not at what is contrary to propriety; listen not to what is contrary to propriety; speak not what is contrary to propriety; make no movement which is contrary to propriety (非禮勿視、非禮勿聽、非禮勿言、非禮勿動)."[8] Traditional Chinese and those rooted in Confucianism are conscious of and practice the don'ts. Another example is, "Do not do unto others what you do

---

4. Julia Po-Wah Tao Lai, "Reconstruction of Traditional Values for Culturally Sensitive Practice," in *Marriage, Divorce, and Remarriage*, eds. Katherine P. H. Young and Anita Y. L. Fok (Hong Kong: Hong Kong University Press, 2005), 276–277.

5. Lai, "Reconstruction of Traditional Values," 278.

6. Lai, 278.

7. Lai, 277–278 and Man and Cheng, 《中國關係學》 [Studies of Chinese Relationship], 12–15.

8. Man and Cheng, 15, 19.

not want done unto you (己所不欲，勿施於人)."[9] This is similar to what the Bible says, "So in everything, do to others what you would have them do to you" (Matt 7:12). The Bible, however, states this in a positive and active manner, whereas Confucius worded it negatively. The don'ts restrict a person from saying too much. Subduing the self enables a person to get along well with others; the flip side is that this contributes to inexpressiveness.[10] When there is disagreement, many traditional Chinese tend to be inexpressive, and to tolerate, compromise, and make concessions even if the other party has wronged them.[11] "I don't agree with you" is not a common statement among these people.

The second phase of practicing *Li* (propriety) is loving others (愛人). Mencius stated that the phase of "loving others" is part of human nature because "all men have natural sympathies; and all men have a sense of pity (惻隱之心，人皆有之)."[12] The path of "loving others" begins with parents and siblings. Family is the starting point to practice *Ren* (benevolence), and then the goal of loving others would be extended to those who are farther from us, unrelated to us, and even to the non-human sphere.[13] Practicing *Li* (propriety) is meaningful, but overdoing it may cause people to bury issues deep in their minds because they are unwilling to open up or to confront others when necessary.

Three Cardinal Guides

In addition to the virtues, Confucianism also encourages its followers to obey the Three Cardinal Guides (三綱). Confucius focused on relationship and connectedness as the essence of human existence, quite different from the individualism and separateness of the West.[14] With community as their priority, the Chinese usually forgo individual interests for the sake of the group. The relationships and value of family, clan, and society of traditional Chinese and those people rooted in Confucianism are very strong with close ties. The Three Cardinal Guides (三綱) were developed in Confucianism in order to maintain social order in the nation, family, and marriage. The Three Cardinal Guides

---

9. Man and Cheng, 15, 19.

10. Lai, "Reconstruction of Traditional Values," 279–283; Man and Cheng, 18–19.

11. Man and Cheng, 16–19.

12. Man and Cheng, 19.

13. Lai, "Reconstruction of Traditional Values," 279–283; Man and Cheng, 《中國關係學》 [Studies of Chinese Relationship], 18–19.

14. Lai, 279–283; Man and Cheng, 18–19.

are: "Ruler Guides the Officials (君為臣綱)," "Father Guides the Son (父為子綱)," and "Husband Guides the Wife (夫為妻綱)."

In accordance with the Three Cardinal Guides, officials are submissive and respectful to their rulers, sons to their fathers, and wives to their husbands. Confucius believed that if every person knew their proper role in family and in society, and fulfilled the related duties and responsibilities properly, social stability and social harmony could be achieved and maintained. When needed, people would be willing to sacrifice or suppress the individual self in order to submit to and obey those in authority over them.

The family unit is like an invisible castle and acts as the safest harbor for all. To many, the most important goal in life is to bring glory and honor to their family. A Chinese saying urges, "Bring honor to one's ancestors (光宗耀祖)."[15] The concept of filial piety has been widely accepted as the paragon of ethics in Chinese society. Chinese tradition rooted in Confucianism is a culture of honor and shame. Confucius believed that only those who are submissive and obedient to parents can become loyal officials and ministers. In the clan, the individual's opinion and honor are not as important as the reputation of the clan. People would sacrifice a talent for the sake of glorifying or benefiting their family and clan. The challenge posed in this kind of society is to maintain a sense of identity and individuality, since greater emphasis is placed on the identity of the family or clan.[16] In a culture of honor and shame, confession is both uncommon and unacceptable because it is considered a shame to reveal personal failure to others, even to relatives or close friends.[17] Therefore, the phrase "I am sorry" is rarely heard in the family.

With regard to marriage, no matter how bad a relationship becomes, a couple may remain silent or inexpressive in order to keep the marriage going and maintain the reputation of the family. Another Chinese saying insists, "Family shames must not be spread around (家醜不得外傳)." Even if the harmony of the marriage only exists on the surface, a couple may maintain customary moral standards, sacrificing their individual interests for the benefit and "face" of the family. To maintain honor, family members subdue their personality and cultivate unlimited patience and perseverance for the sake of family and society.[18] "Face" is a matter of reputation and is interdependent

---

15. Man and Cheng, 17.

16. Lai, "Reconstruction of Traditional Values," 280, 285–286; Man and Cheng, 《中國關係學》 [Studies of Chinese Relationship], 15–20.

17. Augsburger, *Conflict Mediation*, 95–98, 265–267.

18. Lai, "Reconstruction of Traditional Values," 280, 285–286; Man and Cheng, 《中國關係學》 [Studies of Chinese Relationship], 15–20.

on others' face-giving, so mutual tolerance is necessary for living together in Chinese society. A couple recently told me that, although they have been living under the same roof, they have been sleeping in different beds for over twenty years. They have hardly talked to each other over the past few decades. It is a spiritual divorce. They still maintain their marriage, partly because of their children and partly because of reputation, honor, and face-saving. Unfortunately, this is not an isolated example in traditional Chinese society or in other societies with a similar cultural background.

In view of how Confucianism views virtues and relationships, it is not difficult to understand how traditional Chinese deal with conflict and differences. In addition to the traditional thought of "forbear and give in for it is the key meaning of propriety (讓，禮之主也),"[19] Confucius believed that "the person of virtue has no contentions (君子無所爭)."[20] In other words, contention should be avoided. Giving in can result in harmony, and harmony can result in peace and comfort. Avoidance of conflict to achieve harmony is the norm in these societies. Yet, though harmony is an important virtue of Confucianism, Confucius did value differences among people, at least to some degree. He said, "The person of virtue harmonizes but does not conform; the mean person conforms but does not harmonize (君子和而不同，小人同而不和)."[21] Ideally, harmony is not intended to be equated with conformity, and harmony should happen even when there are differences between people. It is a balance between differentiation and integration.

For traditional Chinese, however, far greater emphasis is placed on harmony and public conformity than on difference. When there are unresolved disagreements, they prefer forbearance and perseverance to open discussion. Sometimes, being careful not to hurt others is not simply a matter of being kind but of avoiding bringing the conflict into the open and hurting their dignity or shaming them. While it is regarded as a hallmark of social skill to avoid hurting people's dignity and causing shame, dealing with conflict on the basis of face-saving does not lead to genuine conflict resolution as details of the conflict are rarely discussed.[22] In short, Confucian moral tradition lacks the Western ideal of justice and equality because the highest ideal of Confucianism

---

19. Man and Cheng, 20.

20. Man and Cheng, 20.

21. Lai, "Reconstruction of Traditional Values," 280.

22. David Y. J. Ho, "Face, Social Expectations, and Conflict Avoidance," in *Cross-Cultural Study of Counseling*, eds. John Dawson and Walter Lonner (Hong Kong: Hong Kong University Press, 1974), 248–249, cited in Augsburger, *Conflict Mediation*, 95.

is to become a moral person who is benevolent and loves others harmoniously without focusing on equality, justice, and fairness.[23]

In addition to these virtues and values, it is important to understand how Confucius viewed *Shu* (恕, forgiveness). Someone once asked Confucius about this principle and "whether injury should be recompensed with kindness and virtue (以德報怨, 何如？)," to which Confucius replied, "Recompense injury with straightness, and recompense virtue with virtue (以直報怨, 以德報德)."[24] "Recompensing injury with straightness" means that a person should deal with hurt caused by the offender with integrity, wisdom, and a pure heart, without being influenced by the crookedness within themselves. It also means that when wronged, a person can, with integrity, seek fair recompense and ask for an apology in order to balance justice with forgiveness.[25] As discussed earlier, however, when there is an unresolved conflict resulting in a tension between justice and harmony, traditional Chinese often choose social harmony over a just resolution of the conflict.

Every Chinese knows the saying, "The fewer incidents the better (多一事不如少一事)." When facing conflict, many traditional Chinese prefer less open discussion because it could cause confrontation and disrupt harmony. Even though open discussion can enhance fairness and justice, any disruption of harmony will quickly bring such discussion to an end. If the conflict involves a senior person as the offender, the situation becomes more complicated. A victim who interrupts a conversation or raises an open discussion to address unjust treatment may be considered disrespectful and accused of disrupting harmony. Traditional Chinese and those with a similar cultural background are often expected to compromise, and they find it difficult to view a disagreement as an opportunity in which new concordance can be formed.[26] Therefore, when there is contention, in order to avoid conflict and maintain harmony, they may remain inexpressive, bury the thoughts deep in their minds, and leave the issues unresolved. Choosing to do nothing, they wait with forbearance for the tide to turn. If there is no improvement in the situation, they may lose patience, and the result may be an uncontrollable emotional outburst.[27] This happens not just in secular society but also in many churches, where younger pastors

23. Augsburger, *Conflict Mediation*, 95–97; Lai, "Reconstruction of Traditional Values," 280, 285–286; Man and Cheng, 《中國關係學》 [Studies of Chinese Relationship], 17, 20.

24. Augsburger, 95–97; Lai, 280, 285–286; Man and Cheng, 17, 20.

25. Lai, "Reconstruction of Traditional Values," 283–284.

26. Augsburger, *Conflict Mediation*, 98.

27. Augsburger, 95.

or church members are unable to speak up and have open discussions when the conflicts involve senior pastors or elders.

To sum up, many traditional people perceive and practice relationships and forgiveness through the lens of Confucianism. Accordingly, virtues and values such as harmony, humility, inexpressiveness, community, hierarchy, respectfulness, submission, face-saving, and honor are highly treasured and practiced, even at the expense of equality, justice, and fairness. But harmony at any cost is risky in the long run because true social harmony is only possible when there is a reasonable degree of fairness and justice. Augsburger contends, "No justice, no peace; know justice, know peace."[28] Authentic forgiveness goes beyond social harmony, submission, or face-saving. It involves genuine and in-depth discussion of the conflicts and hurts in order that the offender is given an opportunity to confess and repent, and to be reconciled with the offended. For Jesus says, "If your brother or sister sins, go and point out their fault . . . If they listen to you, you have won them over" (Matt 18:15).

Forgiveness in Western Culture

Apart from the Eastern tradition discussed above, the people of Hong Kong – especially the younger generations and those educated in the West – are greatly influenced by Western individualism, which promotes freedom, fairness, justice, and equality. This section examines how Western culture perceives relationship and forgiveness, how it has shaped people to see the world as being made up of individuals rather than communities, and how it has influenced Christians to see Christianity as solitary rather than communal. It also explores how individualism influences the way Westerners and westernized Chinese people – including parts of the Christian community in Hong Kong – perceive and practice forgiveness as an intrapersonal and unilateral act rather than an interpersonal and mutual transaction emphasizing restoration of relationship.

In Western culture, individualism rules.[29] Individualism places the utmost importance on the individual and promotes the moral worth of the individual. Autonomy, in Western culture, is self-determination. To actualize individuality, individuals are free to shape their lives according to their own views. There are two sides to individualism – good and bad. Augsburger opines that

---

28. David W. Augsburger, email to the author, 5 June 2015.

29. James William McClendon Jr., *Ethics: Systematic Theology, Volume I* (Nashville, TN: Abingdon, 1986), 164.

individualism sets free the human person from being an insignificant atom in the mass of humanity to a responsible agent with dignity, worth, and lasting significance. The idea enters the social mind and we have autonomy idolized, individualism as an "ism" exaggerating self-aggrandizement. So, it is the loss of balance between social responsibility and personal responsibility, between solidarity with others and solitary dignity, that we deplore.[30]

The problem of individualism arises when it is carried to an extreme. When the interests, goals, and desires of the individual take precedence over those of the community, this leads to the separation of people from one another.

Individualism has not only permeated Western societies, it has also influenced the Christian community. Many Christians see themselves living solitary lives rather than in solidarity with Christ and their fellow Christians. James McClendon, in his book *Ethics: Systemic Theology*, warns the Christian community that theology, sociology, and biology do not view the world as being made up of individuals who are separable from all others. He points out that though individualism, collectivism, socialism, capitalism, dictatorships, and anarchies define our times, none of these is faithful to the way of the Torah and Jesus. Human beings are more than individuals, and our true sociality is the community of the church. Christ's church is a community of care that reaches out in love and care to the world (John 3:16; Gal 6:16). There is no solitary Christianity, and the moral life of Christians is a social life.[31] Augsburger contends that this communal sense of Christianity is much closer to "Confucius than to Emanuel Kant, Rene Descartes, John Stuart Mill, and an endless list of Western philosophers that have, since the enlightenment, made each human into an atom of self will and determination, thus creating the idolatry of autonomy."[32]

Because of the Western individualistic preoccupation with self-care, forgiveness has become an intrapersonal process rather than an interpersonal bridge to restore broken relationships. This individualistic culture has adversely influenced the way westernized Chinese people in Hong Kong perceive and deal with forgiveness. Due to various psychological and sociological reasons such as self-love and the understanding of forgiveness as a private act of

---

30. David W. Augsburger, email to the author, 4 November 2016.

31. McClendon, *Ethics: Systematic Theology*, 163–165.

32. Augsburger email to the author, 5 June 2015.

intrapsychic release unrelated to the community, unilateral forgiveness has become the norm.[33]

Individualism does not only influence Western societies to practice unilateral forgiveness, it also taints the way many Western churches – as well as churches in Hong Kong – understand and practice forgiveness as a unilateral act rather than as a social transaction of interpersonal reconciliation. Jones points out that a unilateral act from an individual trivializes forgiveness by making it therapeutically easy. The result is damaging to societies, as well as to Christian community, because victims feel better by simply letting go but with no sense of restoration or reconciliation of broken relationships. Jones also confronts the tendency in churches, as well as in other social contexts, to believe that forgiveness is impossible because violence is the solution.[34] He points out that forgiveness and reconciliation, which are designed to foster and maintain community, have become of little importance for four reasons:

> First, forgiveness has become an increasingly marginal notion. Modernity's emphasis on such themes as individual autonomy, isolated acts rather than character, inevitable progress rather than repentance . . . have all helped to undermine practices of forgiveness . . . [Second], as Christianity has increasingly distanced itself from its Jewish roots and became the established religion in the fourth century, practices and conceptions of forgiveness began to take different shapes. . . . For example, in Western Christianity the confession of sin . . . moved from the community to individualized and increasingly privatized contexts. . . . God's forgiveness became principally an individual transaction between God and a particular person . . . with virtually no consequences for either Christian community or social and political life. . . . [Third], as Christians we have increasingly secularized our own language. . . . Instead of practices of reconciliation, we talk about "managing conflict." . . . We have not been . . . immunized against "therapeutic" language. When forgiveness is seen in primarily individualistic and privatistic terms, we lose sight of its central role in establishing a way of life – not only with our "inner" selves but also in our relations with others. [Fourth, we] emphasize that Christian forgiveness needs to be attentive to and in dialogue with psychological and psychoanalytic concerns if people are to become

---

33. Augsburger, *Helping People Forgive*, 14.
34. Jones, *Embodying Forgiveness*, xv, 5, 37–39.

holy. . . . But, "therapeutic" language has increasingly distorted the grammar of Christian forgiveness. . . . Psychological language and practices have become more powerful than the language and practices of the gospel, not only in the whole culture but even in the Church. In Bonhoeffer's terms, we have substituted cheap grace for the costly grace of discipleship.[35]

These four problems have impoverished the perception and practice of forgiveness in modern Western culture and churches. Similarly, Augsburger points out that the practice of forgiveness in churches nowadays has become a unilateral act from an individual paradigm, rather than a mutual transaction of an interpersonal paradigm. He explains the difference between the two: "The first sets the offended person free by releasing all resentment, all claims for recognition of the injury by the offender, all demands for repentance and restitution; the second is a mutual recognition that repentance is genuine (repentance by one or both parties) and right relationships have been restored."[36] Unilateral forgiveness has permeated Christian community.

Christianity is not solitary. The Christian community should not be directed by individualism. McClendon believes that the communal life of Christians was formed through the covenant meal hosted by Christ at the Lord's Table. Since then, disciples have been connected to one another as community. To maintain community, both Christ's costly forgiveness of human beings and human beings' costly forgiveness of one another are essential.[37] Forgiveness, writes Augsburger, "is not a private act of intrapsychic release but instead a truly social transaction of interpersonal reconciliation. The conflict belongs to the community as well as to the disputants . . . and the understanding of forgiveness is focused on regaining the others as brothers and sisters."[38]

Forgiveness in the Church

This section explores how both Eastern tradition and Western culture adversely influence the way churches in Hong Kong – and in other places with a similar cultural background – perceive and practice forgiveness.

As noted earlier, Hong Kong is an international city, where a person's Eastern roots meet Western culture. In 1841, after the First Opium War, Hong

---

35. Jones, *Embodying Forgiveness*, 37–39.

36. Augsburger, *Helping People Forgive*, 14.

37. McClendon, *Ethics: Systematic Theology*, 232, 241.

38. Augsburger, *Helping People Forgive*, 14.

Kong became a British Colony. Even after 30 June 1997 – when the sovereignty of Hong Kong was transferred back to China from Britain – Hong Kong remains multicultural, and its legal languages continue to be both English and Chinese. Thus, Hong Kong remains closely connected with the Western world.

Since the early 1990s, Hong Kong has become one of the most important financial centers alongside New York, London, and Tokyo. In 2018, its stock exchange was ranked among the top five in terms of market capitalization and total equity raised.[39] Megafirms from mainland China and across the globe come to Hong Kong to set up their offices; they go to its financial market to borrow money and raise capital. Many famous brands and firms from all over the world have opened shops in Hong Kong. Many Westerners have been working in Hong Kong for decades – in various sectors, including retail, catering, banking, and finance – and many Hong Kong Chinese, having studied abroad and experienced Western culture, have returned to live and work in Hong Kong. The official website of the Government of the Hong Kong Special Administrative Region gives the following introduction to Hong Kong:

> Hong Kong is a cosmopolitan metropolis where old tradition blends perfectly with Western culture and post-modern trends. Ethnic Chinese make up the bulk of its population, but there is also a sizeable presence of expatriates and people of different ethnicities. . . . While the waves of Western culture have long arrived on the shores of Hong Kong, traditional values are still held by many Chinese people. . . . Both English and Chinese are the official languages. This bilingualism features in daily life in Hong Kong with many people speaking fluent English. . . . All international newspapers are available in newsstands or convenience shops. . . . While traces of its past can still be found in the fishing villages scattered in its outlying islands, Hong Kong has emerged from a post-war manufacturing base to a major financial and services centre featuring state-of-the-art infrastructure and highly efficient business services. . . . The stock market of Hong Kong provides a wide variety of products ranging from ordinary shares to options, warrants, unit trusts and debt securities. . . .[40]

---

39. ValueWalk, "Top 10 Largest Stock Exchanges in the World by Market Capitalization," accessed 27 May 2019, https://www.valuewalk.com/2019/02/top-10-largest-stock-exchanges/; and Hong Kong Exchange, "Market Statistics 2018," accessed 27 May 2019, https://www.hkex.com.hk/-/media/HKEX-Market/News/News-Release/2018/181221news/181221news.pdf?la=en.

40. Hong Kong Economic and Trade Office, London, "Introducing Hong Kong," accessed 27 May 2019, http://www.hketolondon.gov.hk/intro/hksar.htm.

Hong Kong is a society that has been exposed to and penetrated by global influence and Western culture for decades. Therefore, a Chinese person born and brought up in Hong Kong lives between two cultures, and their perception of relationships, conflict, and forgiveness is influenced by both the East and the West. A Chinese person who subsequently accepts Jesus as his or her savior and becomes part of a local church in Hong Kong would be exposed to the values of a church which has been heavily influenced by Western culture.

Over the last two centuries, Hong Kong has been blessed by missionary church-planting movements from Western countries. Darrell L. Guder, however, points out that in the colonial period the missionary movement was criticized as the insensitive imposition of Western culture on the non-Christian world.[41] This imposition of Western culture on churches in Hong Kong continues today. As discussed earlier, Western churches have been significantly influenced by individualism. Thus, a Chinese person born and brought up in Hong Kong, who subsequently becomes a Christian, would be likely to learn an individualistic view of the practice of forgiveness in addition to the traditional Chinese view on forgiveness.[42]

In the past few decades, most pastors have preached messages of forgiveness that focus on harmony or a unilateral act and release. It is not uncommon to hear the phrase "Do not let the sun go down while you are still angry" (Eph 4:26) being interpreted to mean that a person should bear and resolve their inner hurts by themselves, forgive the offender unilaterally, and let go of their right to justice, leaving this to God. This is seen as an act done for the individual's own good, to free themselves from pain and anger independently of others. Repentance and reconciliation are seldom taught or encouraged, either through fear of disrupting harmony or because of unwillingness to take additional steps to restore broken relationships.

To forgive those who hurt us without a genuine apology and repentance from the offender is not authentic forgiveness. This is "a forgiving heart," "heart willing to forgive," or "a love of your enemy" – an important step, but it is only the first step in Jesus's teaching about authentic forgiveness. By itself, it is damaging to communal well-being, and insufficient to heal people of their

---

41. Darrell L. Guder, "The Church as Missional Community," in *The Community of the Word: Toward an Evangelical Ecclesiology*, eds. Mark Husbands and Daniel J. Treier (Downers Grove, IL: InterVarsity Press, 2005), 115, 118, 123.

42. This phenomenon occurs in many churches in Hong Kong. I have discussed this study with numerous pastors of other churches and seminary professors in Hong Kong. Most, if not all, of them indicated that their church members also tend to practice forgiveness unilaterally, with little emphasis on open discussion of the issues in depth, especially if such discussion would disrupt harmony.

broken past and reconcile impaired relationships to the full extent that God originally intended. God does not merely seek healing for the offended; he requires offenders to face their wrongdoings, confess, and make restitution (Lev 6:1–7; Matt 18:15–17), he expects victims to forgive (Matt 18:21–22), and he desires that both parties be reconciled (Luke 17:3 and Matt 18:15). This should be a social transaction that helps to rebuild the community.

Conclusion

This chapter has discussed two contributory factors that both shape and distort the way Christians in Hong Kong – and in other places with a similar cultural background – view conflict, and perceive and practice forgiveness. These are the influence of the Eastern tradition, primarily Confucianism, and the influence of Western culture, particularly individualism. Given the pervasiveness of Confucianism and the Western individualistic culture, a majority of Christians perceive and practice forgiveness more along these lines rather than as the Bible teaches. Churches must intentionally provide biblical teaching about authentic forgiveness and how it can be practiced within the community. The next chapter gives an overview of several books that examine conflict, sin, hurt, and forgiveness, and the importance of identifying and practicing authentic forgiveness.

3

Broken Relationships: Seven Voices Speak about Forgiveness

Mary's Story

Almost ten years ago, I received an urgent call from Mary, a church member. When I arrived at her home, her mother and younger brother were with her, all of them shocked and deeply saddened. The police had arrested Mary's father. There was a long pause before her mother was even able to tell me the reason for her husband's arrest. He had sexually molested several young children; and when the police searched his computer, they discovered that he was also guilty of child pornography. This had apparently been going on for years. The family members were ashamed, sad, and angry.

Mary's father was a highly respected professional, holding a well-paid senior management post in a big company. When I visited him in jail, I could hardly believe that this highly educated gentleman could really be guilty of such despicable acts. Although he did not talk much during my first few visits, he later admitted that he could not control his desire and lust and had sought release from the pressures of work and bad relationships with his wife and family. What began with pornography had spiraled uncontrollably into child pornography, prostitution, and, finally, luring and forcing children into sexual relationships. Unfaith, pride, concupiscence, and cruelty had taken him down this evil path, where he hurt and destroyed many lives in order to satisfy his desires.

Although I encouraged him to repent of his sins and seek Jesus's forgiveness, Mary's father was so ashamed that he could not believe that Jesus would be willing to forgive him. He told me that he wanted his family members to visit him and forgive him —

but they refused. How could any human being do such evil things? Can someone who commits such evil be forgiven by Jesus, by the offended, and by his own family members?

This chapter examines seven books which deal with the themes of conflict, sin, hurt, and forgiveness. The first two books explore the inevitability and progression of sin, and the fact that sin, conflict, and hurt occur every day. Conflict and hurt are often consequences of sin; but they may also occur when people are acting with good intentions. How people deal with sin, conflict, and hurt will determine whether they will benefit from it or be destroyed by it. The next three books discuss the meaning of authentic forgiveness and confront the way it is trivialized, both in the Chinese tradition of avoiding conflict and in a Western individualistic culture of unilateral action. The last two books focus on the importance of practicing authentic forgiveness and the prerequisites for healing, forgiveness, reconciliation, and "reopening a new future."[1]

The Inevitability of Sin, Conflict, and Hurt

Sin: Radical Evil in Soul and Society *(Ted Peters)*

Ted Peters points out that the Greek words translated "sin" in the New Testament include *hamartia*, meaning "to miss the mark," *adikia*, meaning "injustice" or "unrighteousness," and *anomia*, meaning "lawlessness."[2] The essence of all sin is the unwillingness to acknowledge one's creatureliness and the failure to trust and depend on God. People fail to love God and their neighbors as commanded by Jesus. Instead, they strive to be independent of God and establish their lives on a deceptive foundation. Sin makes them insensitive, unkind, unjust, cruel, and destructive towards their fellow creatures. Whether sinful actions are unintentional – in that people believe they are acting for good, although blindness and self-deceit result in evil actions – or deliberate,[3] they result in conflict and hurt, which is inevitable in life.

Peters describes seven steps to what he calls "radical evil," which constitutes a path progressing from innocence to maximum profanity.[4] The first step is anxiety. Anxiety itself is not sinful, but feeling anxious readies one for sin. The

---

1. I use the phrase "reopen the future" by David Augsburger throughout this book, meaning the reconciliation of a broken relationship so that those involved now have hope of a new relationship ahead of them.

2. Ted Peters, *Sin: Radical Evil in Soul and Society* (Grand Rapids, MI: Eerdmans, 1994), 7–9.

3. Peters, *Sin*, 7–9.

4. Peters, 11–16.

cause of anxiety is the fear of loss. People are tempted to combat anxiety either by pretending that all is well or by striking out preemptively against others by stealing their glory, money, or power. When humiliated, or fearful that others will diminish their sense of worth or their very sense of being, helplessness and rage arise. The ultimate fear is the fear of losing oneself in death. When people feel that their existence is threatened, they are tempted to strike out violently.[5]

The second step is what Peters terms "unfaith." If people lack faith, anxiety will overwhelm them and take control of them, and they may yield to the temptation to strike out in violence. Anxiety and fear will determine their behavior. Lacking faith means not trusting God and neighbor. If people trust the God who created them and sustains them, they will have no fear and will live courageously in the face of anxiety and temptation. They will still feel anxiety, but anxiety will not control their lives. If they trust their neighbors, they are unlikely to hurt them. Where there is no trust, they may indulge in mild sins like gossip; and mild sin, if unchecked, grows. What began as gossip may extend to spreading scandalous rumors or even using illegal means to steal money, possessions, or power that belongs to another.[6]

The third step is pride, which is behaving as if one were God. In doubt, people do not trust God or their neighbors, and so their own egos rule. They conceal their anxiety beneath a blanket of self-control and attempt to exert control over others. Pride does not necessarily mean bragging aloud; it may be manifested as a quiet manipulation of others in the service of one's own psyche. Pride hinders empathy and involvement in the struggles and pain of others. It makes people believe that the world is made up of insiders and outsiders, winners and losers, and that they must always be winners. When facing resistance by outsiders, they – considering themselves insiders – may go to war to eliminate the resistance. Pride often leads to violence.[7]

The fourth step is concupiscence, which encompasses desire, lust, envy, and greed. Desire makes people want to possess what belongs to another. It makes them crave more than what they need to survive, and may even lead to stealing in order to satisfy their desires or protect them from the anxiety of loss. Their desire may be for better or more houses, cars, profit, sexual satisfaction, or power. "It is an unquenchable fire of wanting and wanting and wanting. . . . It comes to expression as . . . seeking profit from someone else's loss, stealing the livelihood from someone who may wither and die because of the theft. . . .

---

5. Peters, 11–12.

6. Peters, 12.

7. Peters, 12–13.

Like a grass fire, concupiscence burns field after field, and there is no hope that it will be extinguished until all fuel is consumed."[8] In the case of Mary's father, the progression of desire and lust to radical sin was intensified by the emptiness of heart caused by pressures of work and the poor relationship with his wife. Although he earned a lot of money, this did not satisfy him; and so he turned to sex to fill the emptiness. However, the belief that possessing more things can satisfy or protect from the anxiety of loss is an illusion. As Jesus said, "You fool! This very night your life will be demanded from you" (Luke 12:20).

The fifth step is self-justification – attempting to portray oneself as righteous, even if it takes a lie or a scapegoat to do so. For example, a guilty child may blame his brother for a missing chocolate or an unfaithful husband may blame his wife for not being attractive enough. Gossip is a common way in which people verbally devalue others – and justify themselves – by accusing them of sins that they have not committed. This happens not only in the secular world, but also in the church – for example, when someone is jealous of another's giftedness. "Self-justification is the denial of our own sinfulness, which is usually accompanied by an ascription of sinfulness to a menacing scapegoat."[9] Self-justification is an expression of unfaith. Those who live in faith are able to acknowledge their goodness as coming from God rather than from themselves and to accept the mixture of good and bad that is found in all people. Therefore, they do not need to find fault with others, and to create and eliminate scapegoats.[10]

The sixth step is cruelty, one of the evil fruits of self-justification. While cruel people can still be sensitive to the feelings of others, they choose to ignore these feelings, justifying their cruelty, and even taking delight in the suffering their victims experience. The cruel person may inflict physical or emotional pain on another – even torture and murder – and enjoy the process. Such cruelty is both irrational and sinful, growing out of the illusion that the anxiety of loss can be eliminated by destroying others.[11]

The seventh and final step is blasphemy, the worst of the seven stages. Peters calls this "radical evil." It manifests itself in two forms: covert and overt. In covert evil, sin comes in the guise of something good, with religious symbols used to enhance a person's position and power. The use of Scripture to justify slavery is one example of covert evil. In overt evil, there is no more hiding.

---

8. Peters, 13–14.

9. Peters, 14.

10. Peters, 14–15.

11. Peters, 15–16.

This is evil in the name of evil, with the conscious use of divine symbols in the worship of Satan. The devil, rather than God, takes central place. Baptism in Christianity that represents life commitment and loyalty to Jesus is replaced by baptism in Satan worship that represents loyalty to Satan; love of neighbor becomes love of self; the Lord's Supper becomes a human sacrifice to Satan rather than Christ's sacrifice on our behalf; and love of enemies becomes revenge against enemies. The relationship between death and life becomes so distorted that killing is confused with living. Ritual cruelty in the worship of Satan is one of the results.[12]

Every day, people are confronted with these sins, in varying degrees, in the workplace, at home, and even in the church – and these may be a result of either the struggles within themselves or the actions of others. There is a war being waged: Will they choose to trust God or their own ego? Will they love their neighbor or themselves? It is crucial for people to know how to fight such sin and evil. In his book *The Prince of Darkness: Radical Evil and the Power of God in History*, Jeffrey Burton Russell writes:

> We are called to fight evil, but we are also called to know how to fight it. Evil is not effectively resisted with hatred and with guns. Evil cannot be defeated with evil, negation with negation, terror with terror, missile with missile. The process of negation must be reversed. Only affirmation can overcome negation; evil can be integrated only by good; hatred can be laid to rest only by love. The only response to evil that has ever worked is the response of Jesus . . . that is to lead a life of love.[13]

We can only combat sin with goodness and love. We are enabled to love because we have first been loved by the Creator. When people realize that they have received the grace of forgiveness, they can borrow from and rest upon the goodness of the forgiver. They no longer need to rely on the illusion of their own goodness. They do not need to put down others to uphold themselves. Peters believes that the most powerful weapons against wrongful acts are the law of love (Matt 5:44; 22:34–40) and forgiveness. In response to radical evil, people must show radical love which is rooted in God, to overcome hatred and hurt; only then can they forgive authentically.[14]

---

12. Peters, 16–17.

13. Jeffrey Burton Russell, *The Prince of Darkness: Radical Evil and the Power of God in History* (Ithaca, NY: Cornell University Press, 1988), 276.

14. Peters, *Sin*, 20–21, 264–265.

A Work of Heart: Understanding How God Shapes Spiritual Leaders (*Reggie McNeal*)

Using six major themes, Reggie McNeal describes how God shapes the hearts of spiritual leaders and develops their lives: culture, call, community, communion, conflict, and the commonplace.[15] It is encouraging to learn that conflict is indeed a major element that shapes our hearts. Some people have the strength of a sensitive heart and the ability to connect deeply and care for others; on the flip side, this renders them vulnerable when exposed to the pain associated with conflict and hurt. Unless they have developed a strategy to deal with such conflict and hurt, they will tend to withdraw from such situations and their hearts will become hardened and their emotions stunted.

Conflict and hurt are inevitable. The presence of conflict does not necessarily imply the displeasure of God. Disagreements sometimes happen, even when people are doing the right things. McNeal cites instances where Jesus and other biblical heroes struggled with conflict even while faithfully following God's will.[16] Moses battled with the strongest king on earth and also had to struggle with his own people, whom God delivered through him. David fought against his enemies to protect and extend Israel's borders and also faced attacks upon his life by his own king, Saul. Paul's ongoing struggle with the opponents of the gospel resulted in him being beaten, stoned, and imprisoned many times, and he also had to deal with sharp disagreements with his own friends and fellow believers (Acts 15). Jesus's love and care for sinners and outcasts prompted many attacks by the Pharisees, and he also had to address arguments among his own disciples. The disciples faithfully evangelized and showed compassion for the needy, and had to face accusations and threats by the authorities (Act 3–4). These examples remind us that, although traditional Chinese and those with a similar cultural background tend to avoid conflict, they do not have to be afraid of conflict which threatens to disrupt harmony. Instead, they must accept that conflict is an inevitable part of life and deal with it proactively and positively.

Conflict strengthens some and destroys others. To benefit from it, one should not merely seek to survive the conflict. McNeal believes that to benefit from conflict it must be welcomed as a heart-shaping tool of God. Chinese tradition encourages people to avoid confrontation and conflict, to keep differences and disagreements within in order to preserve harmony. McNeal

---

15. Reggie McNeal, *A Work of Heart: Understanding How God Shapes Spiritual Leaders* (San Francisco, CA: Jossey-Bass, 2011), 155.

16. McNeal, *Work of Heart*, 155–156.

offers a different view of conflict, presenting it as a means to develop character and enrich, rather than impair, life.[17] He suggests some key steps for being strengthened by conflict.

First, expect conflict. This attitude is important. Pursuing God's mission or being pure in heart does not mean that conflict can be avoided. Conflict and hurt may occur because of differences in values and visions or due to radical evil in the world. No one is immune from being challenged, resisted, mistreated, or even persecuted.

Second, choose which pain and hurt are worth responding to. Trying to please everyone never works. If you are a leader, choose a vision and direction following God's call as purposeless conflict and pain is meaningless and difficult to cope with. Don't create and deal with the conflict for the wrong reason. David did not, nor did Paul and Jesus. They all faced the conflict for the right reasons. David was protecting God's name and land while facing conflict; Paul was spreading gospel for his kingdom while being attacked by the Jews and the Roman Empire; Jesus loved and died for the sinners while facing the unceasing accusation by the Pharisees and the priest.

Third, listen to the critics and take stock of the opposition. When responding to conflict, it is important to discern the genuine concerns that lie behind the criticism and evaluate the motives of the critics.

Fourth, carry out a thorough self-examination. Consider if the critics make a valid point and attempt to understand the opponent's viewpoint. This is never easy because the process of reflection and self-examination can be painful. If the objection has merit, it is important to quickly admit and own the mistake. The ability to do this reflects, and develops, a person's character. Conflict is heart-shaping.

Fifth, get good advice. There are three sources of good advice: godly people, the word of God, and God himself. Godly people challenge us by speaking the truth in love. This is necessary because we are sometimes blinded to what we do that contributes to a conflict. The word of God – particularly sections such as the story of Joseph, the Davidic psalms, Jesus's struggles in the four gospels with religious leaders, and Paul's hardships in the book of Acts – nurture and encourage us when we are in deep pain. When seeking God directly through prayer or meditation during our trials and pain, we may receive healing from hurt (Isa 61:1) or wisdom to face the situation (Jas 1:2–8). Trials result in perseverance and maturity of one's character.

---

17. McNeal, 156, 164.

Sixth, be honest and kind to oneself as well as to one's enemies. When a conflict occurs, there is no need to automatically shoulder all the blame without an appropriate assessment; nor is it healthy to beat oneself up in the face of failure. While honest self-appraisal and appropriate action to rectify a situation are both crucial, it is also important to be kind to oneself. The same approach should be taken with one's enemies. When honesty is not motivated by love, it results in harshness; and this aggravates the situation.

Seventh, forgive and reconcile. If after going through the first six steps, we find out others have wronged and hurt us, then we need to get ready to forgive and reconcile. Authentic forgiveness is a godlike quality that brings blessing to both self and others by releasing those involved from their painful past and allowing everyone to enjoy a new beginning. An unforgiving heart is a cancer of the soul and makes moving forward difficult.

Eighth, allow God access to your heart. Some people become cynical when facing conflict and block themselves from God. But growing through conflict requires a conscious decision to allow God access in order that he might shape the heart.[18] Pastor Andy, whose story was told in chapter 2, made a conscious decision to allow God access to his heart. Although the process has been hard, he has grown through the conflict in his church. He has allowed God to shape him by accepting good advice from mature godly people, reflecting on his own inappropriate emotions and pride, and becoming more aware of, and sensitive to, cultural differences and the need to enhance communication in an appropriate manner, time, and space.

Although conflict is never easy, by dealing appropriately with it, all parties involved can grow and benefit from it.

Jonathan's Story

Another example is about a church leader, Jonathan, who approached me five years ago. He shared the conflict and hurt among pastors while he was developing an outreach ministry in his church. Though the ministry grew very quickly, he was forced to quit. He was deeply hurt. The most difficult thing for Jonathan to accept about his own behavior was that though what he did was right, his way of presenting his stance to his peers and seniors was too harsh and strong. His temper and poor communication skills meant his voice was not heard. Jonathan was advised and guided through the steps above in order to grow through the conflict. The most significant breakthrough was that he was willing to face his weaknesses and allow God to shape him. God reminded him that he needed to

---

18. McNeal, 156–174.

be slow to anger, and Jonathan learned that he could be gentle and yet firm in his stance. Indeed, his new ministry is even larger and more influential than before. The conflict and pain have shaped him to be a more mature and better pastor.

Forgiveness is critical. McNeal states that failure to forgive "binds people to pain and hurt . . . blocks the blessing of God . . . [and the unforgiver] winds up with bitter spirits."[19] He explains that those who do not forgive "see the world and life experiences through victim eyes. . . . What they see is a self-fulfilling scenario of rejection, spiritual entropy, and discouragement."[20] Those who forgive, however, allow God to do radical surgery and rid the heart of the cancer cells of unforgiveness. McNeal also warns that while we "can always afford to forgive, [we] cannot afford not to forgive."[21]

Confronting the Trivialization of Authentic Forgiveness

Forgive and Forget: Healing the Hurts We Don't Deserve *(Lewis B. Smedes)*

Lewis Smedes, at the start of his book *Forgive and Forget*, highlights an important truth: "Deep hurts . . . do not heal with the coming of the sun. . . . Some people are lucky; they seem to have gracious glands that secrete the juices of forgetfulness. . . . But most of us find that the pains of our past keep rolling through our memories, and there's nothing we can do to stop the flow."[22] Smedes believes that if a person refuses to face hurt, that person's life will ultimately be destroyed.

God wants people to forgive. He began by forgiving people, and then he invited people to do the same by forgiving one another. Fairness is natural, but forgiveness is not. Fairness means that people should pay for the wrongful acts they commit, but forgiveness involves the power of love to break this natural rule.[23] Smedes carefully differentiates between what forgiving is and what it is not. Forgiving is not forgetting. Forgiving is not excusing. A person forgives precisely because they refuse to excuse someone and seek to hold that person accountable. Forgiving is not the same as smothering conflict, for this may rob the victim of the opportunity to forgive. Accepting people is not forgiving.

---

19. McNeal, 174.

20. McNeal, 175.

21. McNeal, 175.

22. Lewis B. Smedes, *Forgive and Forget: Healing the Hurts We Don't Deserve* (San Francisco, CA: HarperCollins, 2007), xv.

23. Smedes, *Forgive and Forget*, xv–xvi.

People forgive when someone does something unacceptable to them. Forgiving is not tolerance.[24]

Smedes offers remarkable insights regarding hurt. He describes hurt as having three dimensions: personal pain, unfair pain, and deep pain.[25] This three-dimensional pain arises from a wound that can be healed only by forgiveness.

Personal pain means that only the person who has been wronged can extend forgiveness.[26] No one, apart from the victim, has the right to forgive. To claim to forgive a perpetrator when the forgiver was not the one who was hurt cheapens forgiveness.

The second dimension, unfair pain, occurs when a person is hurt unfairly by another.[27] This undeserved or unnecessary pain is unfair. There is a difference between fair pain – such as a mother yelling at her son for slapping his sister – and unfair pain – such as a drug addict yelling at his daughter for asking for food when she is hungry.

Smedes calls the third dimension deep pain. Some hurts – as when someone cuts the queue – are shallow and slight. While these may be annoying or disappointing, they don't merit any action. But deep pain causes hurts that separate the victim from the offender who causes the pain. Such hurts must be addressed.[28]

Ruby's story, related in chapter 1, illustrates the concept of three-dimensional pain. The hurt and pain Ruby experienced as a child was personal, unfair, and deep. It is not difficult to imagine how helpless, sad, and fearful Ruby felt when her father hurt her time and time again. This pain was both personal and deep. In addition, no one could apologize to her on behalf of her father and no one could forgive her father other than Ruby as that would cheapen forgiveness.

The hurt caused by three-dimensional pain may involve disloyalty, betrayal, or brutality. Disloyalty is when a person who is close treats you like a stranger. Betrayal is where someone who is close treats you like an enemy. Brutality is someone, whether close or a stranger, treating you violently.[29]

---

24. Smedes, 38–49.

25. Smedes, 5–19.

26. Smedes, 5–7.

27. Smedes, 7–9.

28. Smedes, 13–15.

29. Smedes, 15–19.

Although Smedes offers remarkable insights on hurt, some of his recommendations actually trivialize authentic forgiveness. Smedes focuses on intrapsychic release that emerges from psychology and therapeutic culture. Paul Tillich, however, believed that genuine forgiveness is participation and reunion that overcomes the power of estrangement and is completed only when people are brought together – in a renewed relationship that is mutually accepting – and reconciled.[30] Smedes responds, "Tillich was wrong. . . . We can have reality even if we do not have the whole of it. . . . We can forgive and be free in our own memories."[31] Smedes internalizes forgiveness within an individual's heart and mind. Unfortunately, Smedes only focuses on therapeutic mindset to heal the hurt, which underplays or even distorts the central practices of Christian forgiveness. Authentic forgiveness should consist of responsibility, repentance and reconciliation. According to Jones, Christian forgiveness must be "embodied in a way of life, a life marked by specific practices that enable us to unlearn patterns of sin, to repent for specific sins, and to foster habits of holy living."[32] None of these appear to be of concern to Smedes, who ignores the question of the sin that caused the hurt and the need for repentance, and states that the purpose of forgiveness is "for our own sakes" and to "free our own memories," and that the steps to forgiveness include "healing ourselves" rather than being healed by God in the process of practicing forgiveness.[33] In Ruby's case, having accepted Jesus eighteen years ago, she prayed often and courageously for years to be able to let go of the hurt caused by her father's molestation. While she experienced God's love and healing, it was not until her father repented with deep remorse and tendered a genuine apology to her that Ruby was deeply healed and the reconciliation with her father was complete. Ruby and her father now enjoy a renewed and transformed relationship.

Further, although Smedes invites people to ask for and put on "magic eyes" with which to have a new way of looking at things – seeing those who hurt them as weak, needy, and fallible[34] – he does not go on to say that they also need to use "magic eyes" to see how God sees them – as sinners who need to repent, to be forgiven, and to be reconciled with God and others.[35] Jones argues that Smedes's therapeutic forgiveness is "divorced from Christian

---

30. Paul Tillich, quoted in Smedes, 30.

31. Smedes, 30.

32. Jones, *Embodying Forgiveness*, 49.

33. Smedes, *Forgive and Forget*, 13, 27, 30.

34. Smedes, 27.

35. Jones, *Embodying Forgiveness*, 48–53.

practices and doctrine . . . and a false compassion without attention to repentance and culpability . . . a failure to exercise a discerning judgment oriented toward graceful reconciliation."[36] In my ten years of teaching and guiding hundreds of Christians to identify and practice authentic forgiveness, I have found that many Christians perceive and practice forgiveness in the way Smedes describes – as a unilateral act that undermines authentic forgiveness. Authentic forgiveness is more than feeling, healing, and health; it is also about responsibility, repentance, and reconciliation. Indeed, we all need magic eyes from God – both to see the offenders as weak, needy, and fallible human beings, who require the grace of God to repent, and to see the victims as sinners, who may also need to repent of wrong reactions or revengeful actions against the offenders. With "magic eyes" from God, Ruby recognized that it was wrong to hurt her father as revenge for what he did to her. Her apology, along with the love and forgiveness she extended to him, broke the curse of the cycle of bitterness and pain.

Embodying Forgiveness: A Theological Analysis *(L. Gregory Jones)*

L. Gregory Jones provides a Christian theological analysis of authentic forgiveness in his book *Embodying Forgiveness: A Theological Analysis*. Jones employs a stereoscopic vision that reorients our understanding about the presuppositions and implications of authentic forgiveness. Apart from this theological analysis, Jones also addresses social, cultural, philosophical, and psychological theories. To confront the tendency to trivialize authentic forgiveness under cultural influences, Jones insists that the Christian doctrine of the Triune God is central to the most truthful and comprehensive account of authentic forgiveness.[37] He states, "While I applaud the growing conviction that forgiveness can become a means of breaking apart cycles of violence, vengeance, and bitterness, I suggest that the issues need to be more carefully situated within the Christian doctrine of the Triune God."[38] Jones resists faulty understandings of forgiveness, challenges the assumption that forgiveness does not involve accountability, and insists that one cannot separate forgiveness from justice.[39]

---

36. Jones, 52–53.
37. Jones, xiii–xiv.
38. Jones, xi.
39. Jones, xi.

Authentic forgiveness is more than absolution of guilt. Based on the Trinitarian idea that God is a communal being, Jones argues that confession and forgiveness should take place communally. God, through his self-giving communion, is willing to bear the cost of forgiveness to restore humanity to communion in his eschatological kingdom. In response, human beings are called to embody forgiveness, with the aim of restoring communion between God and humankind, and with one another, seeking to remember the past truthfully, repair brokenness, heal division, and reconcile relationships.[40]

Jones confronts the tendencies, both in the church and in other social contexts, to see the world either as "lighter" or "darker" than it is. To see the world as lighter than it is means the tendency to trivialize forgiveness by making it therapeutically easy, without dealing with repentance and justice. Dietrich Bonhoeffer polemicized against such "cheap grace."[41] He resisted, among other things, preaching forgiveness without requiring repentance, and communion without confession. Sin cannot be overlooked or forgotten but, instead, must be confronted and judged in the context of forgiveness. To see the world as darker than it is, on the other hand, is to view forgiveness as impossible because violence is seen as the ultimate master of us all.[42]

Jones highlights problems with forgiveness in Western culture. Forgiveness has become a marginal notion with emphasis on "individual autonomy, isolated acts rather than character, an inevitable process rather than repentance, and the fascination with technique."[43] Authentic forgiveness, which is designed to foster repentance, reconciliation, and maintenance of community, is regarded as being of little importance. Confession of sin, which originated as a communal practice, has moved from the community to the private sphere. Both the language and practice of Christian forgiveness have become increasingly secularized, echoing therapeutic language and practice. Our inner selves are more highly valued than relationships with others, and the intrapersonal dimension has become more important to people than the interpersonal dimension.[44] All of these trivialize authentic forgiveness. As Jones puts it: "Therapeutic language has increasingly distorted the grammar of Christian forgiveness.... Psychological language and practices have become more powerful than the language and practices of the gospel, not only in

---

40. Jones, xii, 163.

41. Dietrich Bonhoeffer, *The Cost of Discipleship* (New York, NY: Macmillan, 1963), 45–47.

42. Jones, *Embodying Forgiveness*, xv.

43. Jones, 37.

44. Jones, 37–39.

the whole culture but even in the church. In Bonhoeffer's terms, Christians have substituted cheap grace for the costly grace of discipleship."[45] Because Westerners and westernized Chinese often internalize hurt and conflict, and seek unilateral healing in order to release personal and deep pain, questions from them about repentance and reconciliation should not be ignored. They are taught to tell themselves that they should forgive the offenders in order to heal their hurts that they "feel" they do not deserve, yet without being made aware of the corresponding need for reconciliation. This is the approach taken by Smedes.[46] Authentic forgiveness, however, is much more than a therapeutic approach. As Jones writes, "at the center of Christian forgiveness is the proclamation of God's Kingdom and the call to repentance so that we can live as forgiven and reconciled people with God and with one another."[47]

Jones resists the notions of either grace without judgment or judgment without grace, of either forgiveness without repentance or repentance without forgiveness. Grace without judgment is cheap grace that does not result in transformation of lives; judgment without grace holds others accountable but results in unbroken cycles of violence. Forgiveness without repentance invites continuity of sin, while repentance without forgiveness can lead to despair and self-destruction.[48] To confront the tendency to trivialize authentic forgiveness, Jones asserts, "When we fail to see and embody this forgiveness in relation to particular lives, specific situations, and concrete practices, we too easily transmute the notions of judgment and grace, forgiveness and repentance, into abstractions that destroy rather than give life."[49] These truths are particularly applicable to the context of the traditional Chinese, who tend to avoid facing conflict, and pursuing accountability and justice, in order to maintain harmony. Eventually, such avoidance becomes life-destructive rather than life-giving.

Helping People Forgive (David W. Augsburger)

Augsburger, in his book *Helping People Forgive*, asks questions about forgiveness: What exactly is forgiveness? Is forgiveness optional? What is the connection between forgiveness, repentance, and reconciliation? A major paradigmatic shift occurred two thousand years ago, when Jesus taught about

---

45. Jones, 39.
46. Jones, 47.
47. Jones, 51.
48. Jones, 135–137.
49. Jones, 136.

forgiveness which allows people to repudiate their past and alter their future.[50] Augsburger states, "Forgiveness allows us to change our minds, begin again, and risk further relationship. . . . This breaking of the cycle of blind retaliation or judicial retribution allows persons, relationships, or institutions to start over, to begin again."[51]

Augsburger believes that as the ideal self has undergone a major change, from modernism to postmodernism, a therapeutic sensibility now takes precedence over a moral sensibility.[52] In other words, in postmodern times, people are encouraged to act on the basis of their own desires, needs, and feelings rather than on the basis of integrity and morality. This can result in rudeness, crudeness, immorality, and even crime. If human beings are to live in community, their natures and feelings must be subordinated to integrity and morality as the proper standard of human maturity.[53] Forgiveness requires a moral context.

As Western culture has become increasingly individualized, the importance of a moral context has been trivialized and forgiveness has often been reduced to passive forbearance. It is only when moral values and virtues are central to the meaning of personhood that the importance of forgiveness is appreciated. Augsburger writes: "Authentic forgiveness is that cluster of motivations which seeks to regain the brother and the sister in reconciliation. . . . The courage to forgive is an excellency of character, a virtue that enables one to act in restoration of personal relationships, to risk in reconstruction of social networks, to commit oneself to live in moral integrity."[54] Forgiveness demands the moral virtues of justice, fairness, love, mercy, repentance, and reconciliation.[55]

To traditional Chinese Christians, and those with a similar cultural background, moral integrity, virtues, and the reconstruction of social networks are highly valued. The pursuit of justice, fairness, and repentance, however, is a challenge as these may disrupt harmony, cause a loss of face, and fail to achieve anything good, from their perspective. To westernized Christians in Hong Kong or elsewhere, the challenge is to subordinate their feelings to moral

---

50. Augsburger, *Helping People Forgive*, ix, 5–7, 9.
51. Augsburger, 9–10.
52. Augsburger, 103.
53. Augsburger, 103.
54. Augsburger, 115–116.
55. Augsburger, 114–115.

integrity and take risks in the reconstruction of community in spite of ever-growing individualism.

Augsburger stresses that forgiveness should not become a unilateral act based on an individual paradigm but a mutual transaction based on an interpersonal paradigm.[56] In both the Hebrew and Christian Scriptures (Gen 42–45; Matt 18:15–17), forgiveness is related to the restoration of right relationships. This forgiveness is not a private act of intrapsychic release but a truly social transaction of interpersonal reconciliation. In Christian tradition, repentance and reconstruction of right relationship are central to the process of forgiveness. According to Augsburger, repentance should consist of three dimensions: remorse, restitution, and renewal. Remorse, when accompanied by a full detailed discussion of the issues, is a genuine sorrow. Restitution is an attempt by the offender to restore what was destroyed, again, when accompanied by full discussion. Renewal is a change in life direction, with the offender not only repudiating past behavior but affirming a new principle of moral action is needed. Forgiveness is the mutual recognition that repentance is intended, embraced, and pursued.[57] Forgiveness is not unconditional. Augsburger writes: "Love may be unconditional, forgiveness is not. . . . The familiar teaching of unconditional, unilateral forgiveness is not forgiving but a return to loving. . . . Forgiveness . . . recognizes the complexity of reopening the future in risk, restoring relationship in trust, and recreating the nature of that alliance in justice."[58] Thus, forgiveness without repentance and reconciliation is incomplete; it is simply love for one's enemy and a willing heart to forgive.

The practice of authentic forgiveness becomes possible when victims retell their story repeatedly, until they are able to separate themselves from their anger and reframe the meaning of the issues involved in a more freeing way. As the telling becomes less of a lament or complaint, victims are gradually enabled to distance themselves emotionally from the injury caused by the issues, to have a desire to discuss the issues, to dismiss some less crucial demands, and to acknowledge the loss and then let it go. Taking the risk of reopening the relationship allows trust to regerminate, which in turn encourages further risking and trusting when (and if and only if) there is response and reciprocal risking and trusting by the other side. This process goes on and on, and each side continues to evaluate the other's trustworthiness when risking more. Am I willing to risk more? Can I trust you more? "The two, trust and risk, go

---

56. Augsburger, 14–16.

57. Augsburger, 14–16.

58. Augsburger, 16.

hand in hand. Risk, in reality, is prior to trust."[59] As risk and trust increase, and when both sides begin to appreciate the other's perspective and victims sense that there is genuine repentance as well as respect, they are better able to appreciate the sincerity of the offender's apology, repentance, and longing for reconciliation. Gradually, both sides recognize that authentic forgiveness begins to occur.[60]

Practicing authentic forgiveness is more than just freeing oneself from bitterness, grief, anger, exhaustion, and fatigued memory. Rather, it is a transaction that brings healing and closure to past situations of failure, choosing to forgo future mistrust and suspicion, and determining to be with one another despite the injury suffered and the alienation experienced. Telling one's story becomes a healing narrative. Since each person belongs to a larger community, individual life stories are framed within a larger communal story, and this gives each person an identity. Authentic forgiveness is grounded in the healing story of two parties involved in a common and connective story that they share with each other in a community of reconciliation. The healing narrative releases a person from the bonds of their old binding story of resentment, self-destruction, distortions, and violence, and begins a new, open-ended story of grace and forgiveness.[61]

The true meaning of a person's story is not found in just that individual but in the larger story of a community. People need a larger and greater story than their own narrative, one that can overcome their persistent self-deceit, redeem their communal lives, develop their character, and express the virtues of justice, courage, love, mercy, and forgiveness. This larger and greater story offers them moral content to live better lives. The narrative of a community draws people together, builds bridges to reconnect the breaches, and invites reconciliation.[62] This happens frequently at Jachin Church when members listen to each other's stories and then begin to practice authentic forgiveness themselves.

Recently, sessions on authentic forgiveness were conducted for a small group at Jachin Church. Group members were encouraged to meet with their enemies in order to forgive and seek reconciliation. Initially, many were resistant to the idea. But a few weeks later, a woman named Sophie boldly shared a story of forgiveness and reconciliation that amazed the group.

---

59. Augsburger, 43.
60. Augsburger, 43.
61. Augsburger, 117–121, 125.
62. Augsburger, 117–121, 125.

Sophie's Story

Sophie's parents had both passed away when she was a teenager, and she had to enter a juvenile home. Her life was made even more miserable by another teenager there who bullied her unmercifully. Sophie had not met this "enemy" for over ten years, yet she continued to carry this deep hurt in her heart. Following the sessions on authentic forgiveness, Sophie contacted her enemy and arranged to meet with her. Over lunch, the two ladies talked about what had happened in the past. By God's grace, Sophie was able to offer forgiveness and, ultimately, there was reconciliation between them. Sophie told the group that although she had initially been reluctant to meet with her enemy, she was grateful that she had taken the risk to do so.

Sophie's story touched the whole group and inspired others to risk practicing authentic forgiveness. In postmodern times, where feelings and emotions are emphasized, storytelling helps to unite people and to reconcile them with one another and with God. Augsburger says that a person's story "must be greater than any social, communal, or national narrative. It is a faith story, an eternal narrative of the meaning of our existence. Only such a story can reconcile us to ourselves, to each other, and to God, who is author of all reconciliation."[63] The forgiving community exists within the story of God's forgiveness. Augsburger contends, "To be a participant in a reconciling community is our highest experience of being human and the one undeniable evidence that God is in our midst."[64]

Healing and Restoration of Relationship by Authentic Forgiveness

Exclusion and Embrace: A Theological Exploration of Identity, Otherness, and Reconciliation (Miroslav Volf)

Born in Osijek, Croatia, Miroslav Volf is a theologian in what was formerly Yugoslavia. He uses two extremes, exclusion and embrace, to theologically explore identity, otherness, and reconciliation. Much of his work emerges out of his reflection on the war that took place in his country. Volf asserts that just as God "donates" the divine self for the godless, in order to receive them into divine communion through the cross of Jesus Christ (Rom 5:6), we should

---

63. Augsburger, 121.
64. Augsburger, 164.

also self-donate for the sake of others – even our enemies – and provide space for others to come in.[65]

In a conflict, people often experience exclusion. Exclusion is problematic because it cuts the bonds that connect the conflicted parties. Cutting the bonds occurs when a person sees the other as one's otherness and an enemy who must be pushed away from one's own self and identity. People are thus separated. Exclusion then eventually leads to an erasing of the separation between them in that the person no longer even recognizes the other as someone who, in his or her otherness, belongs to the pattern of interdependence. One either assimilates the other party or subjugates the other party to one's self. Then, the other party no longer has his or her own identity.[66] Volf explains:

> The other then emerges as an inferior being who must either be assimilated by being made like the self or be subjugated to the self. Exclusion takes place when the violence of expulsion, assimilation, or subjugation and the indifference of abandonment replace the dynamics of taking in and keeping out as well as the mutuality of giving and receiving. . . . Boundaries are part of the creative process of differentiation. For without boundaries there would be no discrete identities, and without discrete identities there could be no relation to the other.[67]

The ultimate exclusion is ethnic cleansing.

Volf proposes embrace as a theological response to exclusion. He takes sin and hurt very seriously when addressing the issue of forgiveness and reconciliation through embrace. Volf asks the difficult question of how one can be loyal "both to the demand of the oppressed for justice and to the gift of forgiveness that the Crucified offered to the perpetrators."[68] In times of conflict, the question is how one can bring justice to the victim while embracing the perpetrator. To Volf, embrace, meaning full reconciliation, cannot happen until the truth has been revealed and justice done. To move from exclusion to embrace, four central concepts are analyzed: repentance, forgiveness, making space in oneself for the other, and healing of memory.[69] Unlike Smedes, Volf

---

65. Miroslav Volf, *Exclusion and Embrace: A Theological Exploration of Identity, Otherness, and Reconciliation* (Nashville, TN: Abingdon, 1996), 23–24, 130–131.

66. Volf, *Exclusion and Embrace*, 57, 67.

67. Volf, 67.

68. Volf, 9.

69. Volf, 9, 29, 100.

is serious about dealing with sin. Several points made by Volf are of particular importance to our discussion on authentic forgiveness.

Volf does not underplay repentance. He believes that "repentance implies not merely a recognition that one has made a bad mistake, but that one has sinned."[70] Since Jesus did not come to call the righteous but sinners (Mark 2:17), admitting one's sin is important for real repentance. Volf argues that both the oppressors and the oppressed need to repent. The oppressed suffer at the sinful hands of others, but they also commit sins of their own. They have to be released from the understandable, but nonetheless inhuman, hatred that has captured their hearts. To repent means to let God establish a new order of his reign in their hearts and to resist sinful values and practices that seek to seduce them. Volf points out that "if victims do not repent today, they will become perpetrators tomorrow who, in their self-deceit, will seek to exculpate their misdeeds on account of their own victimization."[71] Many of those who are oppressed need to repent because they often mimic their oppressors' behaviors, being shaped themselves by the mirror image of their enemies, and they excuse their own reactive behavior by claiming that it is necessary.[72] Volf makes an important point about forgiveness and justice:

> The very idea of forgiveness implies an affirmation of justice. The Lord's Prayer makes this plain. . . . We imply that we owe God something and that other people owe us something. What we owe and what is owed to us can be established only by applying the principle of justice. Hence, no justice, no forgiveness. But if justice, then why forgiveness? Because strict restorative justice can never be satisfied. . . . Nothing can rectify the original offense. . . . Forgiveness is not a substitute for justice. Forgiveness is no mere discharge of a victim's angry resentment and no mere assuaging of a perpetrator's remorseful anguish. . . . On the contrary, every act of forgiveness enthrones justice; it draws attention to its violation precisely by offering to forego its claims. Only those who are forgiven and who are willing to forgive will be capable of relentlessly pursuing justice without falling into the temptation to pervert it into injustice, we could add.[73]

---

70. Volf, 113.
71. Volf, 117.
72. Volf, 113–114, 116–117.
73. Volf, 122–123.

Before pursuing justice, it is important to have a willing heart to forgive, so that pain and hatred do not tempt the oppressed to act unjustly in their pursuit of justice. In many cases, it is impossible to rectify the original offense, and having a willing heart to forgive acts as a safeguard against seeking revenge. How does a person have a willing heart to forgive and abate their desire for revenge so that they can practice authentic forgiveness and pursue justice? Volf suggests:

> By placing unattended rage before God we place both our unjust enemy and our own vengeful self face to face with a God who loves and does justice. Hidden in the dark chambers of our hearts and nourished by the system of darkness, hate grows and seeks to infest everything with its hellish will to exclusion. In the light of the justice and love of God, however, hate recedes and the seed is planted for the miracle of forgiveness. Forgiveness flounders because I exclude the enemy from the community of humans even as I exclude myself from the community of sinners. . . . In the presence of God, our rage over injustice may give way to forgiveness, which in turn will make the search for justice for all possible.[74]

Unlike Smedes's magic eyes, which make no mention of God's intervention, Volf's way to practice authentic forgiveness is in God, with God, and with the other. The offended needs to seek the light of God in the midst of the pain and hurt, and by such light, they can see their enemy and their vengeful self. Through God's eyes they can nourish the seed of forgiveness. Moreover, authentic forgiveness creates a space for the other to restore broken communion as "forgiveness is the boundary between exclusion and embrace. It heals the wounds that the power-acts of exclusion have inflicted and breaks down the dividing wall of hostility. . . . Forgiveness . . . is a passage leading to embrace."[75] Only in the mysterious presence of God would people who have been sinned against and sustained hurt be willing to surrender their hatred and revenge to a God of love and justice. This makes authentic forgiveness possible and practical.

---

74. Volf, 124.
75. Volf, 125–126.

The New Freedom of Forgiveness *(David W. Augsburger)*

Augsburger argues that forgiveness is not denial that allows someone to pretend that all is well, memory fatigue that takes place when a person is exhausted by anger and hatred, or a self-centered goal that seeks only one's own inner peace. True forgiveness is a painful journey, a prolonged wrestling with a wound, and a process aimed at achieving genuine repentance by the offender, graceful acceptance by the victim, and restoration of the broken relationship.[76] This is true forgiveness in the biblical sense.

To "forgive" those who hurt us without genuine repentance by the offender is not true forgiveness. Augsburger writes that it is how a person finds "a mystery of a forgiving heart while the other person in the drama goes another way."[77] Augsburger writes that a victim's forgiving heart is focused on an inner battle between raging against the offender and letting go and being healed. This forgiving heart is only the first step of Jesus's teaching about true forgiveness. It is the "love of our neighbors" and the "love of our enemies" which together form the foundation of forgiveness. Forgiveness requires going beyond the forgiving heart and inviting repentance, risking the self in restoring the relationship. Seeing the other person as having real worth again and seeking to restore perceptions of love are the two feet required in order to walk toward forgiving. True forgiveness is a process, and this process begins with taking whatever steps possible "toward attempting to restore, reconstruct, and rediscover a relationship."[78] Jesus commanded his disciples to go to the other person to rebuke, to forgive, and to reconcile (Matt 5:23–24; 18:15, 21–35; Luke 17:3).[79]

Confronting the trivialization of true forgiveness under the influence of an individualistic culture, Augsburger also describes what true forgiveness is not. It is not something you do to yourself for your own good, to free yourself from pain or to cease being a victim; forgiveness is not taking control so that you can refuse to be held hostage emotionally by an event or person and can focus your energies on the future; forgiveness is not something you have the power to choose independently of the other's attitudes or actions; forgiveness is not merely a refusal to accept injustice as inevitable or tolerable; forgiveness is not offered simply as a release from self-absorption and self-destruction; forgiveness is not a private ritual of release where there is no atonement and no power to bring about reconciliation. None of these things are true forgiveness;

---

76. Augsburger, *New Freedom of Forgiveness*, 17.

77. Augsburger, 14.

78. Augsburger, 26.

79. Augsburger, 17, 25–26.

nevertheless, they are important because they offer wisdom about letting go of being in control of the relationship, the situation, and the hurt, and they are helpful in moving victims toward healing. These are prerequisites for authentic forgiveness because they form "the groundwork of restoring attitudes of love on which forgiveness will stand if it is to ever happen."[80] Further, as Augsburger points out, authentic forgiveness is risking something more than restoring attitudes of love. It is risking a return to conversation and trust, and a resumption of relationship. Forgiveness is more about reconciliation than about love. Forgiveness, in the New Testament, means "to release or set free" and "to offer a gift of grace" in a relational manner, addressing actual interactions among the parties involved.[81]

Forgiving is not an instant solution or a quick fix. It is a long, deep, difficult, and painful process of wrestling with the injury, and risking a return to conversation and a resumption of relationship. The Christ of the cross, who shows how costly it is for God to forgive, is our great example (1 Pet 2:21).[82] Augsburger states, "God used the Cross to make forgiveness possible and to model forgiving to an unforgiving world."[83]

To those who wonder whether or not they should forgive, Augsburger's view is that there is no better alternative than to forgive. To begin with, to exact repayment from the oppressor is often not possible, especially for offenses such as rape or bullying. In addition, not only is exacting revenge stooping to the level of the enemy but the injury persists within. Hidden hatred is self-destructive, and turns our trust and faith in others into suspicion and cold cynicism. Burying the bitterness only paralyzes the mind and soul, freezing reason and emotion. Those who need forgiveness should not hesitate to forgive. Forgiving and being forgiven are two sides of a coin (Matt 6:14–15; 18:21–35).[84]

Some ask *when* authentic forgiveness is achieved. Augsburger states, "Grace and truth, acceptance and confrontation, sacrifice and prophetic rebuke are needed in resolving alienation, injustice, or interpersonal injuries."[85] Authentic forgiveness requires one party to repent and the other party to have the grace to accept that repentance with trust and respect. Authentic forgiveness occurs when there is mutual recognition that both repentance and acceptance are

---

80. Augsburger, 29.
81. Augsburger, 27–29.
82. Augsburger, 29–30.
83. Augsburger, 30.
84. Augsburger, 18–21.
85. Augsburger, 32.

genuine, and when the severed relationship is mended. The final stage in authentic forgiveness is when the victim reconnects with the offender and discovers that the strange chemistry of reconciliation can heal the wound until nothing remains but the remembered scar with a transformed meaning. Such forgiveness results in a deeper and stronger union than before.[86]

Authentic forgiveness, with mutual recognition of genuine repentance, has many implications in cultures where confession is not a usual practice. Where disclosure of a fault may disrupt harmony and result in loss of face – especially for a senior person – issues of conflict and hurt are often not dealt with. Where it is not customary to discuss issues in depth in order to seek reconciliation, people may seek to restore love by a one-sided offering of grace rather than through authentic forgiveness.

When can we give up striving for authentic forgiveness? The answer is *never*. Augsburger believes that seeking authentic forgiveness "is not an optional goal. It is the central task, and when it is not possible, we grieve, feel the loss, experience the failure of relationship, talk about it with a surrogate . . . and reach out for reconciliation."[87] While it may not always be viable to achieve authentic forgiveness, it is important to keep striving for it. There are occasions where it is not possible to achieve authentic forgiveness. For instance, even though the offended grieves and reaches out in love that fully embraces the offender regardless of the offense, the offender may be unrepentant. Authentic forgiveness is also not possible if either party has passed away, cannot be contacted, or is too sad to face the wound. When this happens, the desired goal of healing and reuniting cannot be achieved. In such situations, the offended party (or the offender) needs to accept and grieve the failure and give the situation to God, confessing the longing for authentic forgiveness but accepting that it is no longer possible. Another example is where the offender repents and reaches out for reconciliation but the offended refuses to forgive and reconcile. In such a case, the offender grieves the unwillingness to be forgiven, reaffirms love for the offended, while praying for God's forgiveness.

Since all people are fallen and broken in one way or another, full and complete forgiveness is not always possible. No part of the reconciliation process can be forced. One can only invite. Nevertheless, invitation is the most powerful form of communication. While it is not possible to control the other party's response, a person can be faithful in reaching out, offering genuine confession and repentance – or acceptance and love – and inviting

---

86. Augsburger, 32.

87. Augsburger, 26.

communication and connection. If the invitation is refused, or if the other's response is partial or conditional, one grieves and reaffirms love of the other.[88] Forgiveness is not a single act or decision but a process that takes time; it consists of a series of concrete steps – which are discussed in more detail in chapter 5.

To forgive and restore relationship is seldom easy. In the case of Mary, whose story was told at the beginning of the chapter, it took months before the family members could bring themselves to talk to her father. When visiting her father in jail, I led him to confess his sins and accept Jesus as his Savior and Redeemer. Months after, he confessed his sins during trial in the court, and he was sentenced to jail for twelve years. He has been in the process of repentance and renewal while in jail. Authentic forgiveness requires truth, confession of sin, repentance, judgment and grace. For a long time he did not allow me to visit him after his sentencing. But after a few years, to my surprise, I received a letter from him saying that he was sorry for what he had done. He told me that he had finished reading the whole Bible a few times and completed a masters of Christian Studies through distance learning. His faith in Jesus has been growing gradually though there have been many ups and downs. It is still a long way for him to be transformed. Have the offended and the family members offered any forgiveness to him? I do not know how the offended responded to his confession and sentence, but I know that the family members are still very upset and have yet to forgive him. I pray that all of them can begin a new life. His wife accepted Jesus as her personal Savior soon after he was caught, but the process of forgiveness and reconciliation could be very long.

Conclusion

The books reviewed above answer the question asked at the beginning of this chapter: Can someone who commits radical sins be forgiven by Jesus, the offended, and his own family members? God, through his self-giving communion, is willing to bear the cost of forgiveness to restore humanity to communion in his eschatological kingdom. Our response to God's restoration is to confess and repent, and this is discussed in greater detail in the next chapter. Authentic forgiveness begins with Jesus who forgives us; we, in turn, as followers of Jesus, are called to embody forgiveness that is aimed at restoring communion between God and humankind, and with one another.

---

88. David W. Augsburger, email to the author, 15 March 2017.

Chapter 3 has discussed the progression of sin and the necessity of forgiving and being forgiven, of loving and being loved, when dealing with conflict, sin, and hurt. It has emphasized the importance of practicing authentic forgiveness and confronting its trivialization by cultural influences. The next chapter examines the theological and biblical foundation of authentic forgiveness.

4

Foundations of Authentic Forgiveness

As seen in the stories of Ruby, Jonathan, and Mary, authentic forgiveness is more than just a phrase, a feeling, or even an action; it is a process – sometimes, a very long process. From a theological and biblical perspective, authentic forgiveness is a mutual transaction of an interpersonal paradigm and a restoration of right relationships. Repentance and reconstruction of relationship are central to the process of forgiveness that leads to true and complete healing of relationship. This chapter explores the theological and biblical foundations of authentic forgiveness. It first considers the theological foundations: our God who wills communion and forgiveness, and Christian forgiveness as a communion with God and with one another. Healing of relationship begins with forgiveness and finds completion in communion. The second part of the chapter examines the biblical foundations of the relationship between repentance and forgiveness in the Old and New Testaments. This relationship is important because human sin cannot be overlooked or forgotten; it can only be forgiven when it is confronted and dealt with.[1] Finally, the chapter explores the biblical foundation of genuine repentance – comprising remorse, restitution and renewal – and reconciliation, the pursuit of justice, and love of enemy.

Authentic forgiveness is a mutual recognition that repentance is genuine and reconciliation has been achieved. Without repentance, authentic forgiveness offered by the victim cannot be consummated because the victim can only extend a forgiving heart, which indeed demonstrates a love of one's neighbor and enemy. The incidents of Joseph and his brothers (Genesis 37–45),

---

1. Jones, *Embodying Forgiveness*, xv, 5, 13–15.

the prodigal son (Luke 15), and the Scriptures of Leviticus 6, Matthew 5, 6 and 18, Luke 6 and 17, John 14–16 and 20, and Ephesians 4 are used to draw different principles for practicing authentic forgiveness.

Theological Foundation

God is not self-enclosed. God is one, but he has revealed himself as a Trinity of Father, Son, and Holy Spirit. In the Trinity, Father, Son, and Holy Spirit relate to one another as persons who share an unbounded communion of mutual love and "harmonic difference." "The harmony of Trinity is therefore not the harmony of a finished totality but a 'musical harmony of infinity.'"[2] Within the Trinity, God is ever self-giving. According to Scripture, God is love (1 John 4:8). Love is the nature of God, and so his self-giving is a giving of love. Love requires otherness in order to give and to receive. Thus, the Triune God wills a relationship of eternal, perfect, self-giving, receiving, and loving communion.[3]

The God Who Wills Communion and Forgiveness

The giving and receiving of love is not only among Father, Son, and Holy Spirit, for the Triune God also loves those whom he has created. The Triune God not only wills communion among himself, he also wills communion with his creation. Thus, God created human beings in the divine image and likeness: "Let us make mankind in our image, in our likeness, so that they may rule over the fish in the sea and the birds in the sky, over the livestock and all the wild animals, and over all the creatures that move along the ground. So God created mankind in his own image, in the image of God he created them; male and female he created them" (Gen 1:26–27).

Christian Forgiveness as Communion with God and One Another

Since they are created in God's image and likeness, human beings are destined for loving communion with God and with one another. As God is neither isolated nor self-enclosed, human beings created in his image and likeness are also not made to live in isolation or as self-enclosed individuals. Human beings, however, have rejected their creatureliness and refused – and continue to refuse – such loving communion with God, with one another, and with God's

---

2. John Milbank, *Theology and Social Theory* (Oxford: Blackwell, 1990), 424.

3. Jones, *Embodying Forgiveness*, 113.

creation. Jones states: "We do so when we believe that violence and domination or being dominated, not communion, is our only destiny; we do so when we evade or deny our complicity in habits and histories of sin and evil; we do so when we pretend that those habits and histories are not really so bad after all; and we do so when we even interpret our status as creatures *not* as a sign of communion with our Creator."[4]

Although created and destined for self-giving and receiving, human beings fail to give and receive freely from one another due to self-centeredness, anxiety, and concupiscence. Instead, they may steal from others and strike out in violence; when they fail to trust God, their own egos rule and they seek to exert control over others; they may covet others' possessions to satisfy their own desires, lust, and greed; they may lie or belittle others to make themselves appear righteous. People are trapped in the cyclical habits of sin, evil, violence, and revenge from which they cannot break away.[5] To break out of this cycle requires repentance, forgiveness, and restoration of communion with God and with one another.

The restoration of our communion, however, depends not on human initiative but on God's gracious will and initiative for communion with his creation through his Son Jesus Christ. Karl Barth describes this: "God reveals His own glory in the world in the incarnation of His Son by taking to Himself the radical neediness of the world, i.e., by undertaking to do Himself what world cannot do, arresting, reversing its course to the abyss."[6] God's self-giving love finds expression in the life, death, and resurrection of Jesus Christ, which initiated forgiveness, the restoration of communion with God and with one another, and inaugurated the inbreaking of the kingdom of God. This shows how "God's desire for communion with Creation leads God, as a sign of mercy, to draw human history into God's life."[7]

Jesus did not allow himself to be defined by the experience of being oppressed, betrayed, and abandoned. Refusing to perpetuate the cycle of evil, revenge, and violence, he broke this cycle of sin by his forgiveness. For the follower of Jesus, the only appropriate response to God's forgiveness is to "embody" this forgiveness as a new way of life.[8] Jones explains that

---

4. Jones, 114.

5. Jones, 115.

6. Karl Barth, *Church Dogmatics* IV/1, tr. G. W. Bromiley (Edinburgh: Clark, 1956), 213.

7. Jones, *Embodying Forgiveness*, 119.

8. Jones, 117–121.

those who are forgiven by Jesus are called to embody that forgiven-ness in the new life signified by communion with Jesus and with other disciples. Indeed, that forgiven-ness calls believers to live penitent lives that seek to reconstruct human relationships in the service of holiness of heart and life. For Jesus, forgiveness cannot be earned, whether through repentance or by any other means. But our repentance is the only adequate response to God's forgiveness.[9]

God does not abandon godless sinners but, as Volf expresses it, "donates" the divine self even for sinners and enemies in order to receive them into divine communion through the cross of Jesus Christ and his atonement (Rom 5:6, 10). Through the cross, God demonstrates that he does not want human beings to remain his enemies and he creates space for the offenders to come in. Commenting on the larger narrative of God's dealings with humanity, Volf states:

> Humanity belongs to God and God will not be God without humanity. While human beings were enemies, they were reconciled to God through the death of His son. The cross is the giving up of God's self in order not to give up on humanity; it is the consequence of God's desire to break the power of human enmity without violence and receive human beings into divine communion.[10]

Similarly, in baptism, an individual is identified with Christ in his death and so puts to death whatever belongs to the sinful nature. To die to self is to live for God and others – not just those inside the self-enclosed community but also giving of oneself to those who are enemies. Volf comments,

> By the Spirit we are not only baptized into one body but also made "a new creation." Hence the Spirit ... sets us on the road to becoming truly catholic personalities. ... In the Eucharist, then, we celebrate the giving of the self to the other and the receiving of the other into the self that the triune God has undertaken in the passion of Christ and that we are called and empowered to live such giving and receiving out in a conflict-ridden world.[11]

---

9. Jones, 121.
10. Volf, *Exclusion and Embrace*, 126.
11. Volf, 130.

Disciples of Jesus are called to live according to the pattern of life and death modeled by their master. They are to make space for others to come in, embody forgiveness which reflects the fullness of God's triune communion, and, by the power of the Holy Spirit, be faithful witnesses to God's inbreaking kingdom. In this way, they are able to break the cycles of sin and revenge and restore communion with God and others.

Biblical Foundation

This section explores how forgiveness and repentance are related, and the difference Jesus has made – by his incarnation, death, and resurrection – in the relationship between forgiveness and repentance. Many pastors and Christians tend to trivialize forgiveness by treating it as a unilateral act, without engaging in discussion, requiring genuine repentance, or seeking reconciliation of the broken relationship. The fact that Jesus forgives all by the cross is often misinterpreted, being taken to mean that there are no prerequisites to be fulfilled by the sinner. This section examines how Jesus practiced forgiveness and considers whether Jesus's forgiveness requires repentance by the offender.

The Relationship between Forgiveness and Repentance

Repentance is a crucial prerequisite for sinners to receive forgiveness. Some misinterpret a few Scripture verses that seem to suggest that Jesus proclaimed forgiveness without requesting that sinners repent. For example, Jesus offered forgiveness to a paralytic without requesting repentance of this man (Luke 5:17–26). Jesus prayed from the cross, "Father, forgive them, for they do not know what they are doing" (Luke 23:34). But does this mean that Jesus's forgiveness has no cost? Or does Jesus require that sinners repent?

Jesus began his ministry by preaching, "Repent, for the kingdom of heaven has come near" (Matt 4:17). His ministry was shaped both by the command that sinners repent and by the proclamation and enactment of God's inbreaking kingdom. When Jesus offered forgiveness to the paralytic (Luke 5:17–26), he was not addressing the issue of whether or not forgiveness required repentance but revealing his authority and power as God to forgive sin. This is evident by the response of the scribes and Pharisees, who immediately ask, "Who is this fellow who speaks blasphemy? Who can forgive sins but God alone?" (Luke 5:21). Jesus's response – "Which is easier: to say, 'Your sins are forgiven,' or to say, 'Get up and walk'?" (Luke 5:23) – and his action in healing the paralytic demonstrates his authority to forgive sins (Luke 5:24).

Subsequently, in Luke 5:27–32, Jesus explained that the reason he came was to call sinners. Luke's gospel frequently describes how Jesus welcomes sinners, eats with them, and reaches out to them.[12] But Jesus's ultimate mission is to call sinners to repent; in his own words: "I have not come to call the righteous, but sinners to repentance" (Luke 5:32). This is also illustrated in the parables of the lost sheep, the lost coin, and the lost son (Luke 15:1–32), as well in the encounter with Zacchaeus (Luke 19:1–10).

Luke 15 begins with the parable of the lost sheep and the parable of the lost coin, followed by the parable of the lost son, which is well known as the prodigal son story. When preaching on the three parables in Luke 15, many preachers stress the lavish love of God, who tirelessly seeks the lost. This is true. When the scribes and Pharisees criticized him for spending so much time welcoming sinners and eating with them (Luke 15:1–2), Jesus used these parables to portray God's heart for the lost. It is not easy to understand how the shepherd could leave ninety-nine sheep at risk in the wilderness to seek only one lost sheep, or why the woman made such a big effort to find only one tiny coin and was so happy to celebrate with her neighbors when she found it. Nowhere in Scripture are we told that the shepherd asked someone else to look after the ninety-nine sheep or that the woman was so poor that she needed to use all her effort to find only one little coin. The shepherd and the woman – in going beyond what is rational in their seeking after what is lost and in their celebration when the lost is found – demonstrate this deep desire and unwavering commitment to seek and restore the lost.

The parables' emphases are not merely the finding of the two objects, but more importantly, the subjects of the lost souls. The key themes of the three parables are lost, found, and rejoice (Luke 15:6–7, 9–10, 23–24, 32). The most important aspects of the lost being found are the repentance of the sinner and the subsequent joy in heaven, for Jesus said, "I tell you that in the same way there will be more rejoicing in heaven over one sinner who repents than over ninety-nine righteous persons who do not need to repent," and "In the same way, I tell you, there is rejoicing in the presence of the angels of God over one sinner who repents" (Luke 15:7, 10).

While the first two parables illustrate how deeply God is concerned for, and committed to, seeking the lost, it is the repentance of the lost that causes great joy in heaven. Being "found" is not a physical phenomenon, but an inner life phenomenon of the repentance and transformation of the sinner. The necessity of repentance on the part of the lost is made clear in the parable of

---

12. Jones, *Embodying Forgiveness*, 102.

the prodigal son, and such repentance completes what the parables want to tell us – the lost is found.

How God finds a lost person is far more complex than the way a shepherd finds a lost sheep or a woman finds a lost coin. The parable of the prodigal son, building on the previous two parables, elaborates on how God's grace and the sinner's repentance together result in salvation. Nothing in the parables suggest that the lost sheep or the lost coin were bad or guilty or responsible for their lost condition; but the younger son, in the third parable, was guilty and responsible for his own lostness. The father is there at the beginning and end of the story, and his love towards both his sons was extravagant. Though the younger son dishonored his father – by requesting his inheritance even before his father's death and then squandering it – his father still longed for, and waited for, his son to return.

A turning point in the parable is the younger son's realization of his plight. When famine came and he had nothing to eat except the food given to unclean pigs (Lev 11:7–8), he is sobered by his downfall. He decides to go back home and rehearses how he will approach his father: "Father, I have sinned against heaven and against you. I am no longer worthy to be called your son; make me like one of your hired servants" (Luke 15:18–19). This confession demonstrates the younger son's repentance in humbly placing his future in his father's hands, requesting only that he be treated as a slave. To ask for nothing but the grace and mercy of his father shows his genuine repentance with humble contrition. Seeing his son at a distance, the father does not wait for him to walk up to the house but runs to him – a culturally inappropriate gesture for a father at that time. He welcomed him and lavished gifts upon him, embraced and kissed him, and restored his son to full honor by giving him the best robe, a ring, sandals, and a celebration feast. This warm welcome was especially inappropriate because this son had been so unfilial. The parable shows that God's grace goes beyond human reason and demonstrates God's unrestrained joy over the repentance of the lost (Luke 15:24).

The parable is also about the older son. His father's acceptance and celebration of the younger son's repentance made the older son angry and bitter, causing him to question his father's justice and fairness (Luke 15:29–30). Despite his father's explanations and pleading, the older son refused to accept how precious the return and repentance of the sinner was. Although the father affirms the joy of finding what was lost (Luke 15:32), the story ends without the reader being told whether or not the older son repented of his pride and envy, and whether or not there was reconciliation between the older son and the father and between the two sons. The son who ran away from home at the beginning was within the father's grace by the end of the story, whereas the son who had always been "in" was, in the end, "out."[13] The parable shows that repentance and reconciliation are crucial in order to be "in."

The first two parables show that repentance causes joy in heaven; the third parable expresses what repentance is. Repentance includes remorse, restitution, and renewal. The younger son showed remorse when he returned to his father and confessed that he had sinned. Restitution and renewal are evident in his humble contrition and plea to be taken back as nothing but a slave. This was all he could do – be a slave in order to show his contrition. In all three parables, Jesus stresses the importance of repentance: "there will be more rejoicing in heaven over one sinner who repents" (Luke 15:7); "there is rejoicing in the presence of the angels of God over one sinner who repents" (Luke 15:10); and "Father, I have sinned against heaven and against you" (Luke 15:21).

The importance of restitution and renewal is also evident in Jesus's encounter with Zacchaeus. Tax collectors were regarded as "sinners" (Luke 19:7) because they frequently over-charged taxes and kept part of the monies for themselves. Zacchaeus, as a wealthy chief tax collector, admitted that he had defrauded many people (Luke 19:8). Jesus, heedless of others' opinions, remained faithful to his mission to seek the lost (Luke 19:10) and even invited himself to stay at Zacchaeus's home. This remarkable invitation to communion with a sinner prompted Zacchaeus to repent and resolve to right his wrongs. He demonstrated that his repentance was genuine and proved himself a renewed man by promising to give half his possessions to the poor and to repay, fourfold, those whom he had cheated (Luke 19:8). Zacchaeus's repentance was expressed not with a mere apology but with restitution and renewal. Repentance with actions completes true forgiveness.

Jesus's cry from the cross, "Father, forgive them, for they do not know what they are doing" (Luke 23:34), has often been misinterpreted to mean that he requires no repentance from sinners. But Jesus's words echo the Old Testament practice of sacrifice for unintentional sin (see Num 15:27–31). His words confirm that his death is a once-and-for-all sacrifice to offer divine forgiveness for those people who act wrongly in ignorance. Nevertheless, this wrongful act in ignorance does not mean that there is no requirement of repentance.

In Acts 3:13–19, Peter stresses that people who deny God in ignorance also need to repent. To those who denied, rejected, or even killed Jesus, Peter

---

13. D. L. Bock, *Luke: The NIV Application Commentary* (Grand Rapids, MI: Zondervan, 1996), 406–416.

said, "Repent, then, and turn to God, so that your sins may be wiped out, that times of refreshing may come from the Lord" (Acts 3:19). Luke describes how Jesus, after his resurrection, reminded the disciples that everything written about him in Israel's Scriptures must be fulfilled (Luke 24:44–46) and then authorized them to go to all nations to preach "repentance for the forgiveness of sins" (Luke 24:47). In obedience to this commission, Peter, filled with the Holy Spirit, preached powerfully about the gospel of repentance for the forgiveness of sins: "Repent and be baptized, every one of you, in the name of Jesus Christ for the forgiveness of your sins" (Acts 2:38).[14] Repentance is essential for God's forgiveness of sin and for salvation.

To summarize the above discussion, repentance is indeed a necessary response to divine forgiveness and the salvation offered by Jesus. This is crucial because when disciples are called to follow Jesus to embody forgiveness, they will consider how repentance is associated with forgiveness in Jesus's eyes. Many people tend to trivialize victimization by ignoring the claims of victims if they interpret what Jesus does for us as "cheap grace" – to use Bonhoeffer's term. Cheap grace must be rejected because the forgiveness offered by Jesus was very costly – indeed, it cost Jesus his life. And Jesus takes very seriously the offenses that human beings commit against God and against one another, and he requires that sinners repent.

Jesus's Incarnation Changed the Relationship between Forgiveness and Repentance

Both the Old and New Testaments portray a forgiving God. In the Old Testament, the Israelites repeatedly experienced God's forgiveness and loving kindness, both as a nation (Lev 16:29–34; Isa 54:8) and as individuals (Ps 51). Repentance before God and making restitution to their victims were the first steps in seeking forgiveness (Lev 6:1–7; Num 5:5–7).[15] But after Jesus's death and resurrection, there is a change in the way his disciples are expected to practice authentic forgiveness. Jones explains the significance of Jesus's incarnation and ministry:

> It seems clear that Jesus's proclamation of the Kingdom transforms the relationship between repentance and forgiveness by stressing the gracious priority of forgiveness. . . . In the Synoptic Gospels Jesus's ministry is inaugurated with his announcement of the

---

14. Jones, *Embodying Forgiveness*, 102–103.

15. Jones, 108–109.

Kingdom and his call to repentance (Matthew 4:17). But it does suggest that Jesus's message and actions implied, and sometimes explicitly claimed, a transformed understanding of the relationship between forgiveness and repentance – a repentance contextualized within the announcement of God's inbreaking Kingdom. Thus repentance comes to be situated within Jesus's overall announcement and enactment of God's costly forgiveness.[16]

The gracious priority of forgiveness means that, unlike in the Old Testament, repentance is no longer the first step in the practice of authentic forgiveness. This has significant implications for Jesus's disciples should they consider following him by embodying forgiveness because it means that they must have willing hearts to forgive before they pursue confession, repentance, and justice from others. Volf explains that only those who already have willing hearts to forgive can pursue justice properly; otherwise, it is all too easy to pervert the pursuit of justice due to their own hurt, hatred, bitterness, and passion for revenge.[17]

The gracious priority of forgiveness means that the offended should be willing to forgive even before repentance and justice are obtained. A willing heart to forgive is a crucial first step in the process of authentic forgiveness, and the genuine repentance of the offender is a necessary response to such forgiveness offered in advance by the offended – together, these complete authentic forgiveness and enable the parties to enter once again into a loving, giving, and receiving communion with God and with one another. If, however, the offended unilaterally extends forgiveness and sweeps the offense under the carpet without requesting the offender to repent – perhaps through fear of the cost, conflict, and complications involved or purely for the purpose of self-healing – then forgiveness and reconciliation is inauthentic and the offended has sabotaged the process of authentic forgiveness.

As explained earlier, the harmony sought by traditional Chinese, and those with a similar background, in times of conflict does not necessarily embody forgiveness. Further, the tendency to avoid conflict results in the victim being less motivated to discuss the issues in depth with the offender in order to work towards resolution. The biblical model of offering forgiveness before seeking confession and repentance from the offender would encourage such victims to uphold harmony on the one hand, while also motivating them to reach out to

---

16. Jones, 110.

17. Volf, *Exclusion and Embrace*, 123.

the offender with the willingness to forgive. Thereafter, the victims can pursue justice, seek the offender's repentance, and finally, reconcile.

Remorse, Restitution, and Renewal

This section examines the biblical foundations for three important dimensions of repentance in Christian tradition: remorse, restitution, and renewal. It also discusses reconciliation, the pursuit of justice and fairness, and the love of enemies.

A Story from the Scriptures: Joseph and His Brothers

When it comes to forgiveness, the story of Joseph and his brothers is a touchstone passage. Augsburger contends, "It is the essential theme of the Hebrew Scriptures' teaching on forgiving and it embodies the Jewish understanding of reconciliation of broken relationships as the deeper essence of forgiving. It is not simply an attitudinal shift but a behavioral transformation and change that requires struggle and repentance."[18]

The conflict between Joseph and his brothers began with Joseph's complaint to his father Jacob about his brothers, and because Jacob loved Joseph more than any of his other children and favored him over his brothers – even giving him a special robe as a sign of his favor. As a result, Joseph's brothers hated him. Their jealousy and hatred grew when Joseph told them about his two dreams, in which all the brothers and even his parents bowed down to him (Gen 37:1–11). The brothers allowed their own envy and pride to take control. But if they had trusted God, they would have let God take control; and had they done so, they would have been secure enough not to harm Joseph. Instead, the brothers decided to resolve their hatred and envy by following their own evil ways. Their lack of faith in God and lack of trust in their neighbor – in this case, Joseph – led them to trust in themselves, rather than God, and act violently. It is only by having faith in God that people can live with courage, fearless in the face of harm and able to resist sinning in times of temptation.[19] Peters points out that "the temptation to strike out violently evaporates for a person of faith. Faith is the alternative to sin."[20] With faith in God, people may still struggle with feelings of anxiety, jealousy, and hatred, but these feelings will not be able to control them.

---

18. David W. Augsburger, email to the author, 20 February 2017.
19. Peters, *Sin*, 12.
20. Peters, 65.

Pride determines where a person puts their faith. Pride refuses to allow God to be God. When people follow their own egos instead of God, their pride leads them to take control as if they were God. When Joseph's brothers lived in unfaith, trusting neither God nor neighbor – in this instance, Joseph – their egos ruled and their pride caused them to exert control over Joseph as if they were God. A key characteristic of a proud person is self-centeredness, which results in a lack of empathy for others as one only loves oneself. Pride produces insensitivity, a desire to dominate and enslave others,[21] and even cruelty if one attempts to make themselves righteous when wronging others.

Cruel people can still be keenly aware of others' sufferings, but they choose to ignore them without feeling remorse. They may even feel sympathy for the victim, yet believe that the victim deserves the pain and even justify making them suffer as a means to achieve a higher end. Cruel people may take delight in watching the suffering of others[22] as Joseph's brothers did.

Joseph's brothers were jealous of their brother, filled with pride, usurping God's authority in exerting control over Joseph, living in a state of unfaith, and cruelly plotting to kill their own brother (Gen 37:12–20). They stripped Joseph of his long robe and threw him into the cistern. Then they sat down to eat their meal, ignoring their brother's suffering in the cistern. Even when Joseph pleaded with them for his life, they ignored his distress and refused to listen (Gen 42:21). Finally, all of them, except Reuben, agreed to sell Joseph as a slave to the Midianite merchants. They showed no remorse for their actions, and made up a story to deceive their father into believing that Joseph had been slaughtered by a wild animal. Even when they saw their father tearing his clothes and mourning for Joseph, they chose to ignore his pain and did not tell him the truth (Gen 37:31–34). They sinned cruelly.

After Joseph was sold to Egypt, he lived as a slave and a prisoner for thirteen years. At age thirty, God gave wisdom to Joseph to interpret the double dreams of Pharaoh as a message from God. The ability to interpret dreams demonstrated that one had wisdom in those days. Pharaoh concluded that the Spirit of God was in Joseph and no one else was as wise as Joseph, so he raised Joseph to a high position to be in charge of all the land of Egypt. God vindicated Joseph. Just as Joseph had interpreted, there were seven years of plenty, followed by seven years of famine in Egypt and the countries around it (Gen 41:38–57). As the famine also spread to Canaan, Jacob sent his sons to Egypt in order to purchase grain. It was by the hand of God that the brothers

---

21. Peters, 87, 96–98.
22. Peters, 15, 194.

encountered Joseph again in this peculiar way, which led to the circumstances resulting in authentic forgiveness.

It is crucial to learn what had happened between Joseph's initial encounter with his brothers in Egypt and the time that Joseph revealed himself and offered his forgiveness to them (Gen 45:5, 7, 15). When Joseph first met his brothers in Egypt, they all bowed down to Joseph. This showed that Joseph did not make up his dreams, which were fulfilled (Gen 42:6). In the initial encounter, Joseph pretended to be a stranger to his brothers, treated them harshly, accused them of being spies, asked for their youngest brother Benjamin to come, and put them into custody for three days. Indeed, Joseph was testing them to see if they had been transformed (Gen 42:15).

After three days of being in custody, Joseph put one of them, Simeon, in jail and told them that if they brought Benjamin to Egypt, Simeon would be released. Joseph wanted to test his brothers to see whether they would treat Benjamin in the same way that he had been treated. His brothers then confessed to one another with remorse in Hebrew, without knowing that Joseph could understand, "Surely we are being punished because of our brother. We saw how distressed he was when he pleaded with us for his life, but we would not listen; that's why this distress has come on us. . . . Now we must give an accounting for his blood" (Gen 42:21–22). This confession demonstrated that the guilt and recriminations experienced by Joseph's brothers for the past thirteen years had enslaved and imprisoned them – no less than when they enslaved and imprisoned Joseph by selling him as a slave, after which he became a prisoner held in jail for years.[23] Their confession of hard-heartedness and bloodguilt brought an emotional response from Joseph, who turned away from them and wept (Gen 42:24).

Despite his emotional response, Joseph had decided to bind Simeon and continue to test his brothers to see if their remorse was authentic. When his brothers went home with guilt and sadness, they were shocked and afraid to discover that all the money they had paid for the grain was still in their sacks. They told Jacob everything and asked for Benjamin for the deliverance of Simeon, but Jacob refused, despite the extreme assurance given by Reuben (Gen 42:37–38).

The severe famine continued for a long time, so Jacob had to ask his sons to buy more grain from Egypt when they were facing starvation again. This time, Judah persuaded Jacob to send Benjamin along with them and offered

---

23. J. H. Walton, *Genesis: The NIV Application Commentary* (Grand Rapids, MI: Zondervan, 2001), 677–702.

himself as personal collateral for Benjamin. He was willing to take all the blame if Benjamin did not return (Gen 43:9). Without any option, Jacob agreed to send Benjamin and asked them to bring extra money and presents to Egypt.

On this second visit to Egypt, they were astonished to be invited as guests at a feast at Joseph's home. They were seated in their birth order. Joseph was setting them up to test them, so he, in full view of all the brothers, gave Benjamin a portion of food five times more than the others (Gen 43:17–18, 33–34). Joseph wanted to see if the preferential treatment given to Benjamin would cause them to respond with jealousy and hatred just as it had done in the past when he himself was favored. To let his brothers have an opportunity to act against Benjamin, Joseph asked his steward to secretly put his silver cup into Benjamin's sack. When they finished the feast and left for Canaan the next morning, Joseph's servants chased them and asked them for the silver cup "stolen" by them. Without knowing the cup was in Benjamin's sack, the brothers proposed to Joseph's steward, "If any of your servants is found to have it, he will die; and the rest of us will become my lord's slaves" (Gen 44:9). The steward replied that only the one found to have the cup would stay and become his slave, and the rest would be set free. This prepared them for the real test as the cup was then found in Benjamin's sack. Joseph was eager to find out whether they would gladly turn against Benjamin, who was now their father's favorite and who had also enjoyed preferential treatment by Joseph at the feast. But they did not. Instead, they tore their clothes, loaded their donkeys, and all returned to the city to meet Joseph. This act was an indication that they had indeed been transformed and renewed.

When they went back to meet Joseph and were asked why they had stolen the cup, Judah indicated that all of them, not only Benjamin, should be held as Joseph's servants because it was their corporate guilt. Then, Joseph wanted to test them one final time to see if they would betray Benjamin and seek their own welfare; he said, "Only the man who was found to have the cup will become my slave. The rest of you, go back to your father in peace" (Gen 44:17). Judah stood up again to defend Benjamin and begged to take the place of Benjamin (Gen 44:18–33). This act – admitting the deed as a corporate guilt and offering to take Benjamin's place – was an act of restitution of the sin they had committed against Joseph many years ago. They could not rectify Joseph's pain and suffering, but they did so when they defended Benjamin, Joseph's brother. Indeed, their restitution was clearly shown again upon their father's death when they asked to be slaves for Joseph to compensate for their deeds (Gen 50:18). Judah's speech here to save and not "sell" Benjamin showed that he was totally renewed when compared to his suggestion to "sell" Joseph previously. Now, the brothers were sensitive not only to Benjamin's feelings, but also to their father's, as they knew that their father had indicated that he would die of sadness if Benjamin did not return. They were all renewed. The miraculous change in the brothers represented by Judah was as incredible as the change in the status of Joseph. It was the work of God.

Having noticed the change in his brothers, Joseph asked all his servants to leave. He could no longer control himself, and he made himself known to his brothers and wept so loudly that many Egyptians heard (Gen 45:1–2). Then, Joseph offered his forgiveness and restoration of communion to his brothers by saying that it was God who sent him to Egypt, so that he could be preserved in order to save many lives. God has the ultimate sovereignty in every human deed. Joseph's forgiveness was clearly offered repeatedly to his brothers upon the death of Jacob. When Jacob passed away, the brothers were afraid that Joseph might hold a grudge against them and pay them back for all their misdeeds to him, so they sent a message to Joseph to admit the sins they had committed to him; they asked Joseph, "Please forgive the sins of the servants of the God of your father" (Gen 50:17). When Joseph heard their message, he wept. The brothers then came and fell down before Joseph and said they were his slaves as restitution for their misdeeds to him. It showed that the brothers acknowledged their misdeeds with remorse, restitution, and renewal, but they had not fully accepted Joseph's forgiveness. Joseph reassured them of his forgiveness and reconciliation once again, "Don't be afraid. Am I in the place of God? You intended to harm me, but God intended it for good to accomplish what is now being done, the saving of many lives. So then, don't be afraid. I will provide for you and your children" (Gen 50:19–21).

Not only did Joseph have a strong sense of God's control over the situation, he also knew that he should not let his pride take control of him and the situation. "Am I in the place of God?" is a question that the offended one should always ask oneself in order not to abuse one's power over the offender. Joseph, being a victim, did not feel self-justified to pay back. Taking revenge is sometimes a mask employed by the victims to act as God's instrument of justice and retribution. This incident shows that authentic forgiveness has two sides. For the offenders, they have to genuinely repent with remorse, restitution, and renewal. For the offended, they have to forgive and reconcile the broken relationship, sometimes with a scar of transformed meaning. Joseph forgave because he submitted to God's sovereignty. He did not merely promise not to harm his brothers, given that he had all the power to seek revenge, but he also welcomed them to stay with him and provided for them and their families.

Authentic forgiveness is a process, and it could be as long and difficult as it was for Joseph. Remorse, restitution, and renewal are the three important dimensions of repentance for the offenders, which are Joseph's brothers in this case. Reconciliation is necessary and biblical to complete authentic forgiveness. Augsburger states, "Joseph's patience and leveling of the field make reconciliation possible. His restoration of love needed to be completely reviewed a second time after his father's death and his brothers renewed anxiety about possible revenge. It demonstrates the process of forgiveness is not quick, clean, simple, but long, sometimes difficult and always complex."[24]

Seven Principles from Scripture

This section considers several Scripture passages – Leviticus 6, Matthew 5, 6 and 18, Luke 6 and 17, John 14–16 and 20, and Ephesians 4 – which give us seven principles for the practice of authentic forgiveness.

Principle 1:

The first principle relates to restitution, renewal, and reconciliation. In Leviticus 6:1–7, God shows that someone who deceives or robs another does not only sin against the victim but also against God. Thus, the guilty party must not only "make restitution in full, add a fifth of the value to it and give it all to the owner," but also, "as a penalty they must bring to the priest, that is, to the Lord, their guilt offering, a ram from the flock, one without defect and of the proper value." The additional amount ("a fifth of the value") was intended to discourage the guilty person from stealing again. Renewal is expressed by changed behavior, that is, not repeating the offense. The righting of one's wrongs is evidence of true repentance – without true repentance there is no forgiveness from God or from others.

Jesus affirms this when he warns his disciples: "Therefore, if you are offering your gift at the altar and there remember that your brother or sister has something against you, leave your gift there in front of the altar. First go and be reconciled to them; then come and offer your gift" (Matt 5:23–24). According to Jesus, offenders cannot ignore their wrongdoing but must attempt to reconcile with the offended before approaching God in worship.

Zacchaeus not only practiced what Scripture requires but went beyond (Luke 19:8). Integrating Leviticus 6:1–7 and Matthew 5:23–24, we learn that those who offend another must proactively seek reconciliation with both God and the offended. They should approach the offended to discuss the details

---

24. David W. Augsburger, email to the author, 15 March 2017.

of the conflict, take responsibility for their wrongdoing, make restitution as fully as possible, show renewal by not repeating the behavior, rebuild the relationship, and reopen the future. Since offenders are also accountable to God, they should ask the Holy Spirit to reveal their sin, and then confess, repent (John 16:8), and seek God's forgiveness and reconciliation.[25]

Principle 2:

The second principle relates to remorse or contrition. Remorse is an essential element in the process of authentic forgiveness. As the palmist writes, "a broken and contrite heart you, God, will not despise" (Ps 51:17). All forgiveness, human or divine, is based on the same paradigm that there is mutual recognition by both parties that (1) contrition and repentance are genuine; and (2) right relationships are restored. Genuine repentance merits uncountable times of repeated forgiveness. As Jesus commanded his disciples, "If your brother or sister . . . repent, forgive them. Even if they sin against you seven times in a day and seven times come back to you saying, 'I repent,' you must forgive them" (Luke 17:3–4).

Principle 3:

The third principle relates to the pursuit of justice. Every act of forgiveness enthrones justice. If the offender does not proactively seek restitution and reconciliation, the victim should reprove the offender. In Matthew 18:15–16, Jesus tells the disciples, "If your brother or sister sins, go and point out their fault, just between the two of you. . . . But if they will not listen, take one or two others along, so that 'every matter may be established by the testimony of two or three witnesses.'" This demonstrates the importance of in-depth discussion of the issue and, where necessary, the presence of others as witnesses which would help avoid self-centered emotion or one-sided accusation.

Jesus goes on to add: "If they [the offenders] still refuse to listen, tell it to the church; and if they refuse to listen even to the church, treat them as you would a pagan or a tax collector" (Matt 18:17). If the offender does not repent, there is a sequence to be followed in confronting the offender – individually, as a group, and ultimately, as a church. The church's role is to help the victim to reprove the offender and pursue justice. If the offender refuses to confess and repent, the church is authorized to treat the offender as an unbeliever and exercise the Father's judgment (Matt 18:18–20).

---

25. R. Gane, *Leviticus: The NIV Application Commentary* (Grand Rapids, MI: Zondervan, 2004), 134–140.

Principle 4:

The fourth principle relates to developing forgiving habits and discovering our similarities by understanding our shared humanity. When Peter asked Jesus how many times he should forgive someone who repeatedly sinned against him, Jesus replied, "seventy-seven times" (Matt 18:21–22) – meaning that our willingness to forgive should have no limit. Jesus elaborated on this with his parable of the merciful master and unmerciful servant (Matt 18:23–35). In this parable, a servant owed his master ten thousand bags of gold and was unable to repay his debt, while another man owed this servant a hundred silver coins and was also unable to repay his debt. The master "took pity on him [the servant], cancelled the debt [of ten thousand bags of gold] and let him go," but the servant then refused to cancel the other man's debt of only a hundred silver coins and "had the man thrown into prison until he could pay the debt." The master called this unmerciful and unforgiving servant "wicked." He challenged the servant's conduct: "Shouldn't you have had mercy on your fellow servant just as I had on you?" and pronounced judgment on him: "In anger his master handed him over to the jailers to be tortured, until he should pay back all he owed." Jesus spells out the principle of this parable: "This is how my heavenly Father will treat each of you unless you forgive your brother or sister from your heart." John Patton, in his book *Is Human Forgiveness Possible?* writes: "The only proper response to [God's forgiving our sins] is our forgiving."[26] Those who have experienced God's mercy and grace should imitate this by offering mercy and grace to those who have wronged them.

Jesus gives a similar principle in the Lord's Prayer and the subsequent verses in the Sermon on the Mount: "Forgive us our debts, as we also have forgiven our debtors," and "For if you forgive other people when they sin against you, your heavenly Father will also forgive you. But if you do not forgive others their sins, your Father will not forgive your sins" (Matt 6:12, 14–15). Patton interprets the Lord's Prayer as an expression of the kingdom, which is experienced in part now and will be experienced fully only in the future. This prayer affirms that our Abba Father expresses forgiveness as a relationship between himself and his children, and that we should also express this forgiveness in our relationships with one another. In the eschatological sense, God's forgiveness and ours may be tendered simultaneously. Some interpret this parallel forgiveness as human forgiveness being a reflection of the divine forgiveness; but theologically, there is a huge difference between

---

26. John Patton, *Is Human Forgiveness Possible?* (Nashville, TN: Abingdon, 1985), 158.

God's forgiveness and ours, since people are not indebted to one another in the same manner and degree to which they are indebted to God.

Patton points out that the basic meaning of the word "forgiveness" in the New Testament is "releasing, surrendering, and letting go,"[27] and that every true disciple of Jesus should develop and embody a forgiving habit that can break away from the cycle of revenge, release others from debt and bondage, and thereby also experience the release of their own debt by God's forgiveness.[28] As disciples are forgiven by God, they should discover that they themselves are debtors, just like those who offend and are in debt to them. As Elijah said, "I am no better than my ancestors" (1 Kgs 19:4). In the incident of the woman who committed adultery (John 8:2–11), when asked if the woman should be stoned to death, Jesus responded, "Let any one of you who is without sin be the first to throw a stone at her" (John 8:7). Not a single person dared to throw a stone, which demonstrated that they understood that no one was without sin. Patton point outs the importance of understanding human forgiveness "not as doing something but as discovering something – that I am more like those who have hurt me than different from them. I am able to forgive when I discover that I am in no position to forgive."[29] Disciples are both grace-receivers and grace-releasers.

Principle 5:

The fifth principle relates to the Holy Spirit's guiding and empowering of the disciples. The awakening to a sense of sin, which then leads to repentance, is often a mystery. Yet this awakening, as in the story of the prodigal son, is the crucial turning point where sinners see their true self – and this requires God's grace, the work of the Holy Spirit, and the sinner's openness. At the Last Supper, Jesus promised that he would not leave his disciples alone but would send the "Advocate" (some versions translate this "Counselor") to teach and remind them of everything he had said to them (John 14:16–26). This Advocate is the Holy Spirit, the Spirit of truth who comes from the Father, testifies for Jesus, guides the disciples into all truth, and discloses to them what is to come (John 15:26–27; 16:12–14).

The resurrected Jesus also linked the Holy Spirit with forgiveness when he said to the disciples, "As the Father has sent me, I am sending you. . . . Receive the Holy Spirit. If you forgive anyone's sins, their sins are forgiven; if you do not

---

27. Patton, *Is Human Forgiveness Possible?*, 161.
28. Patton, 156–161.
29. Patton, 176.

forgive them, they are not forgiven" (John 20:21–23). The Holy Spirit empowers Jesus's disciples to refuse the habit of sins, learn the truth, practice forgiveness, and foster the communion initiated by Jesus. Jones writes:

> There is . . . an inextricable relation between receiving the Holy Spirit and engaging in practices of forgiveness. Indeed, the Spirit works both to turn and re-turn people to the power of Christ's forgiveness and to embody that forgiveness in relations with others. . . . The Spirit enables those who have been forgiven by Christ also to become those who forgive, seeking to restore communion with others in analogous fashion to the ways it has been restored to them. . . . It is the work of the Holy Spirit to guide people in learning how to embody Christ's forgiveness in . . . people's lives.[30]

Principle 6:

The sixth principle relates to a forgiving heart and love for one's enemy. Mutual recognition of the need for genuine confession and repentance is a crucial element leading to authentic forgiveness. Authentic forgiveness cannot happen without a forgiving heart. But a willingness to forgive demonstrates courage, for the victim must fight an inner battle to overcome anger and let God bring healing.[31] This forgiving heart is the first step in Jesus's teaching about forgiveness. This forgiving heart is the first step in Jesus's teaching about forgiveness. It is part of loving your "enemies" (Matt 5:38–45; Luke 6:27–28) as well as loving your "neighbor" (Matt 22:39).

Biblically, love for self and love for neighbor are not two loves but different aspects of the same love. Both are equally precious; and so, in love, one loves oneself and the other equally. The same applies to forgiveness: "For if you forgive other people when they sin against you, your heavenly Father will also forgive you. But if you do not forgive others their sins, your Father will not forgive your sins" (Matt 6:14–15). And in service, "do to others what you would have them do to you" (Matt 7:12). For Christians, nothing on earth is more precious than love. Jesus taught his followers not to "resist an evil person," but instead, when forced "to go one mile, go with them two miles" instead (Matt 5:39–41).

---

30. Jones, *Embodying Forgiveness*, 129–131.
31. Augsburger, *New Freedom of Forgiveness*, 17.

Christian love, *agape*, is a choice beyond feeling, a volition beyond emotion, and a loving beyond liking. Only by redefining love from a worldly understanding to the Christian concept of *agape* can one truly love others. *Agape* is when one loves the unlovely in generous self-giving that is based on the goodness of the lover; it is willing obedience to the commandment to love; it is self-sacrificial and unconditional love that accepts the other regardless of the cost; and it is a love that prizes others as having equal worth.[32] The call to love our enemies is a call to faithful witness to a God who refuses to abandon human beings as enemies but, instead, seeks to transform them into friends.[33] Abandoning one's enemy reflects one's inner conflicts and the dark side of one's soul. By excluding someone, one participates in the creation of one's enemy. The more one knows oneself, the more one knows one's enemy. Forgiving love has the power to include the enemy.

Nelson Mandela, a former South African president, "walked the talk" and loved his enemies. For example, he invited one of his former jailers to a dinner commemorating the twentieth anniversary of his release from prison; he invited his former prison guard to his inauguration ceremony as the South African president; and he even sat down to a meal with the man who tried to kill him. Hate cannot overcome hate. Evil never destroys evil. Only love defeats hate, only goodness overcomes evil.

Christians must imitate Jesus, who taught – by word and example – that only love can defeat hatred and violence (Matt 5:39, 44–45).[34] Christian *agape* can be viewed as benevolence, the foremost among the Five Constant Virtues of Confucianism that traditional Chinese and those with similar cultural background pursue. When an offender refuses to repent, traditional Chinese can be encouraged to respond with *agape* or benevolence – which is no stranger to them – and love their neighbor or even an enemy. This *agape* or benevolence is the foundation and the first crucial step in authentic forgiveness.

Principle 7:

The seventh principle relates to releasing anger and retelling one's story. The Bible does not prohibit anger; indeed, Jesus himself experienced and expressed anger. On one occasion, when some wanted to accuse Jesus for healing on the Sabbath, "he looked around at them in anger" and was "deeply distressed at their stubborn hearts" (Mark 3:5); he angrily rebuked the Pharisees and

---

32. Augsburger, 138–139.

33. Jones, *Embodying Forgiveness*, 262–263, 267.

34. Augsburger, *New Freedom of Forgiveness*, 121, 126.

teachers of the law for their hypocrisy (Matt 23:13–36); and he expressed, in no uncertain terms, his anger against those who had turned his Father's house into a marketplace and hindered the Gentiles from worshiping there (Matt 21:12–13).

Anger is of two types: constructive and destructive. Augsburger points out that

> anger as an emotion is morally neutral, which can be good or bad, and helpful or harmful, depending on the reasons for the anger and how it is exercised. Destructive anger freezes the normal processes of grieving into pathological mourning. Constructive anger seeks to break through the walls, yearns to remove the barriers, presses to open communication, and mobilizes energy to work at injustices.[35]

When Christians are angry about injustice, abuse, poverty, lies, hypocrisy, and the like, this is righteous anger. But when angry, they should be careful not to sin. Paul does not teach against being angry, but he warns against sinning while being angry: "In your anger do not sin" (Eph 4:26). John Stott believes that Ephesians 4:26 promotes righteous anger, but one has to be alert of the danger of misusing anger and causing sin. Therefore, Paul encourages Christians to get rid of unrighteous and undisciplined rage and anger (Eph 4:31). They must not let their anger persist – "Do not let the sun go down while you are still angry" (Eph 4:26) – lest they "give the devil a foothold" (Eph 4:27), meaning that they must not allow the devil any room to operate in their lives.[36] In the hands of the devil, and given our own sinful nature, anger could easily be turned into a self-centered emotion that produces destructive results, both personally and communally.

It is vital to ensure that anger is constructive rather than destructive. Augsburger explains, "Anger and love are compatible. Love without anger is as worthless as anger without love."[37] Thus, it is possible to release anger properly and purposefully, with love and openness. This happens by first owning one's feelings instead of denying the anger and pain. This is demonstrated throughout the Psalms; for example, the psalmist writes, "Save me, O God, for the waters have come up to my neck. . . . many are my enemies without cause, those who seek to destroy me. . . . When I weep and fast, I must endure scorn" (Ps 69:1, 4b, 10).

---

35. Augsburger, 60–62.

36. Snodgrass, *Ephesians*, 249–250.

37. Augsburger, *New Freedom of Forgiveness*, 65.

In addition to releasing anger, it is also critical to tell one's story. First, victims must retell their story of anger, pain, and hurt repeatedly to God, by praying (both written and verbal prayers), and by asking for his justice and deliverance (see Psalms 36, 40, 42, 43, 69, 80, 139). Volf suggests that by placing our unattended anger, our vengeful selves, and an unjust enemy before a God who loves and does justice, our hearts can be nourished by the love of God and the light of justice, rather than by the devil.[38] Next, victims should examine and share their anger and their story with a community of faith, and this group of people must listen and help them to discern the matter (Rom 12:15; Eph 4:16; 6:18). Further, retelling the story repeatedly can help them to separate themselves from anger and pain, and reframe the meaning of the issue. Finally, with a forgiving heart (Matt 5:38–45) and the deliberate decision to leave vengeance to God (Rom 12:19–21), victims must risk going to those with whom they are angry and attempting to straighten out matters (Matt 18:15–17).[39] If the person does not listen, one or two others should be taken along as witnesses. If the offender still refuses to listen, the victim should tell the church. If the offender does listen, however, trust begins to germinate. As trust and genuine repentance grow to a certain level, the victim will be able to appreciate the sincerity of the offender's apology and repentance. Gradually, authentic forgiveness begins to occur.[40]

Conclusion

This chapter has explored the theological and biblical foundations of authentic forgiveness and drawn key principles from the Scriptures that model authentic forgiveness. In the next chapter, these principles are used to develop a ministry plan for churches seeking to help their members identify, practice, and embody authentic forgiveness, and confront any trivialization of it.

---

38. Volf, *Exclusion and Embrace*, 124.
39. Augsburger, *New Freedom of Forgiveness*, 68–69.
40. Augsburger, *Helping People Forgive*, 43.

5

Practice:
A Plan of Action for Your Church

This chapter transitions from theory to practice. After summarizing the key theological and biblical principles described in chapter 4, it explains the theological implications that flow from these principles for a church that takes seriously the call to forgive as Jesus did. The remainder of the chapter outlines a ministry plan, including setting goals and developing strategies, for a church that wishes to help its members identify and practice authentic forgiveness.

Theological Implications

Chapter 4 outlined some key theological and biblical principles of authentic forgiveness. First, the importance of embodying forgiveness, which lies at the heart of the Christian faith. God wills communion and forgiveness. Since human beings are created in God's image and likeness, they were intended to enjoy loving communion with God and with one another. However, conflict, evil, and hurt are inevitable in human life, and human beings are trapped in the cyclical habits of sin, violence, and revenge, thus they break away from God and from one another. The incarnation, death, and resurrection of Jesus, through which he initiated love and forgiveness for us, restores communion. Disciples should imitate Jesus by embodying love, forgiveness and communion with one another as a new habit of life, so as to renew people's minds and rebuild broken relationships. Augsburger writes, "The value of human beings lies in their created worth. The value is affirmed by grace and rooted in creation.

No one is too low to be an object of God's love. No one is excluded from the forgiveness of God, except one excludes himself by unrepentance."[1]

Second, the importance of appreciating that authentic forgiveness comprises both genuine repentance and reconciliation, whereas genuine repentance consists of remorse, restitution and renewal. Nevertheless, if either party chooses to remain inaccessible, unrepentant, or unforgiving, the victim's willingness to forgive or the offender's willingness to repent would still be regarded as genuine even though the process of authentic forgiveness would be incomplete. In such instances, they can but grieve the loss of communion and the inability to reconcile, and continue to seek authentic forgiveness as much as possible so that God can continue to heal, transform, and renew people as well as empower people to rebuild broken relationships.

Third, understanding that every act of forgiveness enthrones justice and proactively pursuing both justice and reconciliation in accordance with the biblically mandated process for doing so. If the offender does not admit his wrongdoings, the offended shall abate his or her passion for revenge and pursue justice by approaching the offender and seeking the confession and repentance of the offender. If the offender does not listen, two or three people from the Christian community should help talk to the offender. If he or she still does not acknowledge their wrongdoing, the church, pastors and leaders, should go. In doing so, the offended is not merely seeking justice, but he or she is also working to let the offender take responsibility and rebuild a real community of faith from the broken relationship.

Finally, prayerful dependence on, and obedience to, the Holy Spirit. This requires being attuned to the Spirit's voice as he reveals the truth, allowing him to soften our hearts so that we may humbly seek forgiveness when we have offended and generously forgive when we have been offended. To listen to the Spirit's voice clearly, one needs to seek a biblical view, seek advice from godly people, retell the story by writing a letter to God and sharing it with godly people, pray for a forgiving heart and a love of his enemy, and pray for a way to biblically deal with the conflict, sin, and hurt. Following these steps puts the offended in a position to seek justice without seeking revenge.

Several theological implications flow from these principles. First, church members should be made aware that authentic forgiveness is a requirement, not an option. When wronged, the offended should respond to the conflict and hurt with authentic forgiveness; only then can hurt become life-transforming.

---

1. Augsburger, *New Freedom of Forgiveness*, 40–41.

Second, church members should model themselves on Jesus. Rather than being hopelessly trapped in cycles of sin, bitterness, hatred, and revenge – where their hearts are frozen, their minds paralyzed, and their emotions destroyed – they must seek the help of the Holy Spirit to break out of these cycles of hopelessness and form a new cycle of love, forgiveness, and communion. As they begin to see that all people are precious and loved by God regardless of their wrongdoing, and as they learn more about the offenders' background and what causes them to act sinfully, they will be helped to view offenders with understanding and mercy. Authentic forgiveness can transform conflict and hurt from being life-destructive to being life-constructive.

Third, church members who are traditional Chinese, or from a similar cultural background, and whose highest values include harmony, avoidance of conflict, and face-saving, need to learn that authentic forgiveness cannot be complete without confession, repentance, and reconciliation. This is necessary to confront their tendency to practice forgiveness by overlooking misdeeds in order to maintain harmony on the surface. Conflicts are not resolved when misdeeds are overlooked – the hurts continue to ache and the relationships continue to decay. As forgiveness enthrones justice, to make harmony genuine, both parties should discuss the issues in depth with one another so that they can confess, repent, and reconcile with substance.

Fourth, church members influenced by a Western individualistic culture must guard against trivializing forgiveness by viewing it as a unilateral act or a means of intrapsychic release which fails to seek repentance and reconciliation. These individuals should seek insight regarding biblical forgiveness in order to confront these fallacies.

Fifth, since authentic forgiveness requires genuine repentance in order to reconcile the parties, if offenders remain unrepentant, the offended should develop Christian *agape* with which to love their enemies. To love one's enemy is to faithfully witness to a God who refuses to abandon human beings as enemies but seeks to transform them into friends. Disciples of Jesus should seek his grace to help them imitate God by loving not only their neighbors but also their enemies.

Six Goals

To become a church where authentic forgiveness is a daily reality, six important goals must be accomplished.

Goal 1: Accept the Inevitability of Conflict

The first goal is to help the congregation accept the fact that conflict and hurt are unavoidable. Conflict and hurt are not instigated by God but are a result of human sin. Some sinful acts are deliberate, others are unintentional. It is the way people choose to respond to sinful acts that determines whether the process and result of forgiveness are life-constructive or life-destructive.

Goal 2: Realize That Forgiveness Is the Best Response

The second goal is help church members realize that the best response to sinful acts is forgiveness. A biblical response is not characterized either by revenge or by hiding the hatred or burying the bitterness. Jesus's disciples are called to fight evil by goodness, affirmation, love, and forgiveness, and not by evil, negation, hatred, or revenge. "Darkness cannot drive out darkness; only light can do that," said Martin Luther King, Jr.[2] By the light and love of Jesus, human hostility and hurt can be healed by human forgiveness.[3] Forgiving and being forgiven are two sides of a coin. In forgiving, not only is the offended released and renewed, the forgiveness extended also frees the offender from guilt and brings reconciliation with the victim.

Goal 3: Understand Authentic Forgiveness

The third goal is to help congregants identify what authentic forgiveness is. They will learn that biblically grounded authentic forgiveness can transform conflict and hurt into a life-enriching experience. Using various Scripture passages – which have been discussed in chapter 4 – they will be shown how God uses authentic forgiveness, comprising both genuine repentance and reconciliation, as a divine tool to heal people's hurt, release them from a painful past, correct their behavior, reopen a new future, and restore broken relationships.

Goal 4: Become Aware of and Confront the Trivialization of Cultural Influences

The fourth goal is to educate church members of how cultural influences – both the Chinese tradition and a Western individualistic culture – may shape their perception and practice of forgiveness, and guide them to confront

---

2. Martin Luther King, Jr., "MLK Quotes," Dr Martin Luther King Jr, accessed 3 June 2019, http://www.drmartinlutherkingjr.com/mlkquotes.htm.

3. Russell, *Prince of Darkness*, 276.

any tendency to trivialize authentic forgiveness. The Chinese tradition rooted in Confucianism upholds values such as harmony, inexpressiveness, humility, avoidance of conflict, honor versus shame, and saving face. Western individualistic cultures value self-love and individual interests over and above the interests of the community.

Goal 5: Practice Authentic Forgiveness

The fifth goal is to teach church members concrete steps that can be taken to practice authentic forgiveness, and guide them to practice such steps. Whether they are the offenders or the offended, they will be encouraged and led to face the wounds of the past by prayerfully recalling how they were wronged or what wrongs they have done to others and then, either to confess and repent or to forgive and initiate reconciliation. The process of authentic forgiveness will go on until their wounds are healed and become a scar with transformed meanings. Such forgiveness results in a deeper and stronger healing and union than before.

Goal 6: Cultivate Authentic Forgiveness as a Way of Life

The final goal is to challenge church members to cultivate authentic forgiveness as a new way of life, with Jesus as their model and the Holy Spirit as their enabler. They need to unlearn their past cyclical habit of blind retaliation or burying the conflict and pain within, and develop a lifelong and daily habit rather than one-time event of forgiving.

Five Strategies

Five key strategies – which Jachin Church has successfully employed for many years with significant results of many lives being transformed and healed – will help achieve the goals discussed above.

Step 1: Preach on Authentic Forgiveness: A Sermon Series

A sermon series is the primary way to communicate the importance of authentic forgiveness to the congregation. Since Scripture plays a continuing and transformative role in the lives of Christians, sermons about forgiveness are used as signposts pointing the congregation to God and his divine gift of authentic forgiveness as a tool to change lives. A variety of Scripture passages will be used to describe God's view of authentic forgiveness and how we are to practice it. Appendix A gives a list of suggested topics and Scripture references.

This teaching from the pulpit should also explain how the characteristics of Chinese tradition rooted in Confucianism and the Western individualistic culture are applicable to your context, in relation to relationships and forgiveness. Contrasts between the norms of these two cultures will be highlighted as the Scriptures are expounded. In particular, the sermon series will focus on confronting the tendency to trivialize authentic forgiveness.

Step 2: Identify Members in Need and Interested in Learning

The pulpit is used to communicate the truth to the congregation so that they can be shaped and transformed by God's word. God, out of his love and mercy, chooses to reveal himself and his truth through his word. However, since the adult congregation is likely to be large and from different backgrounds, in-depth explanations, discussions and the practice of forgiveness will need to take place in smaller groups. Different platforms could be used for this purpose, and groups ranging from ten to one hundred people could be formed to facilitate the process of teaching, guiding, and accompanying people as they go through this journey towards repentance and forgiveness.

For the past nine years, Jachin Church[4] has used various platforms – including a biweekly pastoral cell group, monthly cell leaders' gathering, church school classes, and discipleship training groups – for this purpose. The results have been gratifying, with many lives healed and transformed. Some of Jachin Church's stories are included in this book. Similar results have been obtained when similar methodology was used for other churches and Christian institutes in past years.

Step 3: Practice Authentic Forgiveness

Authentic forgiveness is neither an attitude nor a single act; it is a process. Having learned the theory, those interested in practicing authentic forgiveness need to be guided, step by step, through this process. Based on the theological and biblical principles already discussed, several concrete steps must be taken by both the offenders and the offended.

---

4. At Jachin Church, the congregation ranges from young adults in their early twenties to older adults in their eighties. In relation to their level of education, some congregants have only graduated from secondary school while over fifty percent of congregants have obtained at least a bachelor's degree.

Offenders, who accept their need to be forgiven, should be guided through the following eight steps.

1) Realize the need to proactively resolve the conflicts and hurt.

2) Recall, and then write down in detail, what they have done to hurt others. True guilt – as opposed to guilt arising from an overcritical inner self – is a gift from God, intended to awaken offenders to the reality and gravity of their sin. It deserves to be explored, expressed, and released. Offenders are guided to know that the guilt can be "not undone, but redone through recognition and repentance."[5]

3) Talk to a mature Christian who can walk through the process with them and help them to discern the appropriate way to resolve the conflict, repent, and reconcile.

4) Confess their wrongdoing to the victims – clearly, and in detail. How detailed the confession should be depends on the situation. In a case of defamation, for instance, it should be as detailed as possible; in a case of adultery, it is neither necessary nor helpful to go into great detail of the sins committed. Wisdom must be exercised in regard to how public the confession should be; while this needs to be determined on a case-by-case basis, usually, confession should be as public as the commission of the act. It is also important to be sensitive to the impact on hearers of such a confession.

5) Express their remorse with contrition. This means demonstrating genuine sorrow and involves an in-depth discussion of the details of the matter with victims.

6) Make restitution, as far as is possible.

7) Allow the word of God and the transforming power of the Holy Spirit to begin the work of renewal in their lives – resolving to make a change in their life direction, disavowing old patterns of behavior, and affirming a new principle of moral action.

8) Ask victims for forgiveness, giving them adequate time and space to respond; this could take days or months, or even years, depending on the gravity of the wrongdoing. Offenders must realize that forgiveness is the mutual recognition of both offenders and victims

---

5. Augsburger, *New Freedom of Forgiveness*, 76.

that repentance, comprising remorse, restitution and renewal, is genuine, intended, and embraced.

Victims, who recognize that they need to offer forgiveness, could work through the following eleven steps.

1) Bring the story, hurt, and pain to God as King David did (see Pss 34, 54, 56, 57, 59). Victims may write letters to God, expressing their hurt, and allow themselves to grieve before God.

2) Retell the story repeatedly to God and – when ready to do so – to a mature Christian, perhaps a pastor, lay leader, or counselor. Victims should retell the story repeatedly until they can separate themselves from anger, lament, or complaint. Once they are able to discuss the matter with increasing distance from the injury, the practice of authentic forgiveness becomes possible. Care and sensitivity will need to be exercised by those in whom they confide.

3) With the help of the Holy Spirit, grieve,[6] seek clarity to view the matter clearly, and draw comfort from seeing God's hand in the midst of the pain. The stories of Joseph, King David, and Jesus will serve as reminders that God is with his people in their suffering. For instance, no matter how badly Joseph was treated, the Bible repeatedly affirms that God was with Joseph: "The LORD was with Joseph . . . in the house of his Egyptian master. When his master saw that the LORD was with him . . . the LORD blessed the household of the Egyptian because of Joseph. . . . the LORD was with him . . . and granted him favor in the eyes of the prison warden. . . . The LORD was with Joseph . . ." (Gen 39:2, 3, 5, 21, 23). By taking these first three steps, victims may reach a point where they are enabled to reinterpret the meaning of their hurt and pain. As Joseph says to his brothers when they are finally reconciled, "Do not be distressed and do not be angry with yourselves for selling me here, because it was to save lives that God sent me ahead of you" (Gen 45:5).

---

6. Grief is a necessary process of life when facing pain, loss, change and hurt. To start the process, one needs to face and admit the pain and hurt, rather than ignoring it. To continue, one needs to understand and accept the fact that there will be different and unexpected emotions, such as anger, hatred, false guilt, incapability or withdrawal, which arise during the process of grief. Grief is a process of journeys into the memory of the past before the work of letting go can be complete. In grieving, one leaves the past and turns to the future. The process comes to an end when one can be at peace, willing to take the risk to proceed forward to step 4 and beyond.

4) Release anger by "owning" and "opening." Owning the feelings means not denying them but releasing them properly. Opening means repeatedly opening up one's story to God, to those who are mature in Christ, and, later on, when appropriate, to the offenders. As Volf suggests, victims are to place their unattended anger, their vengeful self, and their unjust enemy before a God who loves and does justice. Let the hearts of the victims be nourished by the love of God and the light of justice, rather than by the devil.[7] As the victims examine and share their anger and their stories, the community of faith must listen with empathy and help them to discern what exactly has happened by separating the emotion from the fact – who is responsible, what exactly have the offenders done wrong, and if the victims have contributed to the matter (Rom 12:15; Eph 4:16; 6:18). Repeated retelling of the story may help victims to gradually separate themselves from anger and pain, and to reframe the meaning of the issue.

5) Discover similarity with the offender by recognizing their own sinfulness. As discussed earlier, forgiveness is not something that victims *do*; rather, it is something that takes place when victims discover that they are more like the offenders than unlike them, more similar than different. They are able to forgive when they discover that they, too, are forgiven by grace. Thus, victims who are grace-receivers should also be grace-releasers.

6) Begin to value and love the offenders once again. This means recognizing that even when the offender has done a terrible wrong, there is more to a person than a single misdeed or even a series of misdeeds. Victims will seek to view the offenders through God's eyes. The value of human beings lies in their created worth; this was affirmed by Jesus's incarnation, death, and resurrection – which was for the sake of every human being, no matter how sinful. No one is too evil to be loved by God, and no one is excluded from the forgiveness of God – except those who exclude themselves by unrepentance.[8]

7) Release their painful past. Like Joseph, King David, Jesus and Paul, victims must accept the reality that the wrong done to them by

---

7. Volf, *Exclusion and Embrace*, 124.
8. Volf, 38–43.

the offender cannot be undone. To accept the past as past is to come to terms with reality, so that they can move forward without continuously looking back. Victims need to believe that offenders are able to repent, change, and turn away from past patterns of behavior. They must also believe that these offenders are equally able to change by the power of the Holy Spirit. During the process of releasing their painful past, victims will revisit the past, retell the story of their injury, and face their loss through reframing and reinterpreting the meanings of the matter.[9]

8) Develop a forgiving heart that is characterized by love of one's enemies by prayerfully entrusting the matter to God (Matt 5:38–45) – especially if the offender is unrepentant. Forgiveness is conditional; but love is not. A victim needs to develop a forgiving heart, to choose deliberately not to seek revenge (leaving the vengeance to God, Rom 12:19–21), and to take the risk of approaching the offender in order to work things out calmly and humbly, not in anger (Matt 18:15–17).[10] Risk taken by the victim has to go hand in hand with trust in the offender. When the victim takes risk to approach the offender and finds that the offender does respond in the right direction, trust will germinate and grow. Gradually, the possibility of authentic forgiveness begins to grow when the victim is able to see the genuineness of the repentance of the offender.[11]

9) Forgive, and begin to reconstruct the relationship. Victims must listen to the offender's confession. They should recall and review the offense, and work through the pain and anger together with the offender. The repentance has to be genuine, honest, and as complete as possible. This is the central work of forgiveness (Matt 18:15; Luke 17:3–4). When both parties recognize that there is genuine repentance and acceptance by the other, they can work together to rebuild the relationship. Forgiving must come before any attempt is made to forget; otherwise, forgetting will be destructive because there is still unhealed anger within the mind.

10) Reopen the future. The unhealed wound is transformed so that it has healing power within the soul. The reopening of the future may

---

9. Augsburger, *Helping People Forgive*, 68–72.

10. Augsburger, *New Freedom of Forgiveness*, 68–69.

11. Augsburger, *Helping People Forgive*, 43.

result in a friendly parting with mutual respect, a willingness to risk another journey, or a new level of friendship.

11) Reaffirm the relationship. Victim and offender ought to celebrate the progress made in their journey towards reconciliation. As the two parties touch each other as deeply as possible to release the pain, they shall mutually recognize and affirm that right relationship has been restored and will grow.[12]

During the practice of authentic forgiveness, if the offender is inaccessible, unrepentant, or deceased, the offended can only grieve as fully as possible and work through the first eight steps. Working through these initial steps will bring them a measure of healing and release from God. Even though there is no complete reconciliation, the victims who have tried to practice authentic forgiveness can experience healing with love, peace and hope.

When practicing steps nine, ten, and eleven, there will be occasions where both parties are responsible – in varying degrees – for the offense. In such instances, to simply say "I forgive you" would not just be inappropriate but could also convey a sense of self-righteousness or superiority. A more fitting response might be, "I want to accept and to be accepted," "I want to be close again," or "I would like to forgive and to be forgiven." Seeking mutual acceptance does not convey a sense of superiority or inferiority and, if expressed lovingly, is powerful in reconciling and restoring relationships (Matt 7:12).

In the case of a marriage relationship, what is frequently required is mutual forgiveness. Seldom is one person either totally to blame or completely innocent. Nevertheless, this does not mean that blame or responsibility is assumed to be fifty-fifty. Authentic forgiveness happens when both are willing to meet the other, work to reconstruct their relationship, and seek to give and receive genuine forgiveness or repentance in relation to the issue in dispute. The result of forgiveness in marriage is to set each other free so that both can live spontaneously, joyfully, fully, openly, and honestly. If one party is willing to forgive, repent, and reconcile, but the other is unresponsive, authentic forgiveness is incomplete; nevertheless, the willing party is still extending an invitation of reconciliation to the other side and doing one's part biblically.

Traditional Chinese families and those with a similar cultural background often avoid conflicts and simply bury the issues. They must be encouraged to discuss issues openly and honestly, and meet with each other in order to work together to reconstruct their relationship. In marriage, the goal is to

---

12. Augsburger, *New Freedom of Forgiveness*, 48–51.

achieve unconditional familial love and respect with five basic freedoms: (1) freedom to "see what one sees" as the more I love you, the more I set you free; (2) freedom to "think one's own thoughts" as respect invites the other party to think individually, without being pressurized to always accept the other's ideas; (3) freedom to "feel one's own feelings" as caring sets the other party free to feel either positive or negative emotions, without being forced to suppress one's own feelings because of fear; (4) freedom to "choose what one wants" as valuing the other one sets one free to respond voluntarily, choose with integrity, and want what one truly wants, without being coerced to submit blindly to other's desire; and (5) freedom to "act, speak, risk and to be real" as prizing the other one sets one free to act responsibly, speak as a real person of integrity, risk living as a genuine person with self, with others and with God.[13]

Step 4: Form Small Focus Groups and Encourage Storytelling

Small focus groups are to be set up to provide follow-up and guidance for people who have learned about authentic forgiveness and have tried to practice it themselves (steps 1, 2, and 3 above) but still need some help. Each focus group should consist of no more than six to eight members. Pastors, with the help of lay leaders, will guide the participants in practicing authentic forgiveness – either to forgive or to be forgiven. A minimum of five two-hour sessions are recommended for this purpose.

At each session, apart from going through the steps outlined in Step 3 above, pastors should also worship with and pray for those in need. In the penultimate session, Holy Communion could be shared so that participants are reminded of, and embraced by, the love and forgiveness of God, and thereby strengthened and empowered to go through the tough process of forgiving others. David Fitch, in his book *The Great Giveaway*, points out that people today pursue experiences of all kinds. Postmodernists learn and engage with truth differently than do those of previous generations. They do not merely want to see truth talked about intellectually, as information; instead, they want to experience, and engage with, truth. They demand a living truth they can participate in. Focus group participants will experience how worship, prayer, and Holy Communion connect them to God as he becomes present in a real

---

13. Augsburger, 86–89, 110–111.

way in the mystery of the Lord's Supper, services of healing, and community worship.[14]

In the small focus groups, pastors will encourage participants to tell their own stories – their experiences of struggling with their wounds and forgiving others – so as to support and encourage one another to keep on trying. In the postmodern era, storytelling is very effective because while people tend to be suspicious of truth that is known to them only in words, they respect truth that can be seen, lived, and experienced in life, and are eager to participate in one another's stories. McClendon says that truth is narrative dependent, and it is to be probed, experienced, and lived out rather than talked out.[15] The power of stories, the wisdom of narrative, and the truth of human experience – conveyed in the accounts of encounter between people and God and between one person and another – can break down walls. By listening to and participating in the stories, the inner self of an individual is awakened.[16] When a person's own story is inadequate, they are hungry for a wider story to complete it, a greater story to overcome their persistent self-deceit and redeem their life in community with other Christians. The Bible is full of wider and greater stories – and as people participate in them, they are character shaping.[17] To inspire church members to practice authentic forgiveness, pastors can share the stories of Joseph and his brothers or the parable of the prodigal son, and especially their own stories of forgiveness – since this would encourage people to share their personal stories too. In doing so, those in need would be awakened, so as to begin to practice authentic forgiveness themselves.

Four years ago, a small discipleship group at Jachin Church was learning about and practicing authentic forgiveness. During these sessions, Agnes shared how she had been deeply hurt.

Agnes's Story

Forty years ago, Agnes left Mainland China and came to Hong Kong – with her mother and two younger siblings – to reunite with her father, who had come to Hong Kong a few years earlier to work and prepare a home for them. The three children were between the ages of eight and twelve at the time. When they arrived in Hong Kong – lost, insecure,

---

14. David Fitch, *The Great Giveaway: Reclaiming the Mission of the Church* (Grand Rapids, MI: Baker Books, 2005), 49, 60–65.

15. McClendon, *Ethics: Systematic Theology*, 77–78, 345.

16. McClendon, 77–78, 345–348.

17. McClendon, 349–351.

and fearful of the new environment – their father avoided them. Then they found out that he had another family. Agnes, her mother, and her siblings were alone in Hong Kong, with hardly any money, no adequate accommodation, and unable to speak Cantonese (the main language spoken in Hong Kong). The whole family was hurt by the father's sin. After her parents' divorce, Agnes and her mother both suffered from serious depression. For forty years, Agnes seldom met her father; neither did her mother or siblings.

After learning about authentic forgiveness, Agnes decided to approach her father, confront him, and seek reconciliation. By God's grace, her eighty-five-year-old father was not only willing but grateful for the opportunity to meet with Agnes and confess his wrongdoing to the family. Agnes's father talked about the hardships he had faced when coming to Hong Kong in the 1970s. Then, in tears, he apologized humbly and sincerely for what he had done to hurt them. After struggling for weeks, Agnes decided to forgive her father and reconcile with him. She also shared the gospel with him. Amazed by the Christlike love his daughter had shown him, Agnes's father decided to give his life to follow Jesus.

When the rest of the group heard Agnes's story, not only were they full of amazement and praise for God, they were also inspired to practice authentic forgiveness in their own lives. Subsequently, many group members experienced breakthroughs in their relationships with offenders. God is faithful!

Step 5: Evaluate the Content and Process

The ministry plan includes both cognitive learning and practice. Evaluation of the content and presentation of both these aspects is important in order to correct shortcomings and make continuous improvements. This can be done through questionnaires, which participants will be requested to complete at the end of a sermon or teaching series and, again, after the focus group sessions. Their feedback may prompt adjustments to make these sessions more effective. Participants' feedback about how the experience has impacted their relationship with God and with others could also be used to encourage others to participate in these sessions. Appendix B provides a sample questionnaire, which you can customize for your own context.

At Jachin Church and other Christian institutes, similar questionnaires have been used with over five hundred participants. The responses received have been overwhelmingly positive – many indicated that they had already begun to practice what they had learned; most said that they would recommend this learning experience to others; and some suggested that a more comprehensive course, over a longer duration, would be useful, since this was a difficult topic. The positive responses received have shown that people are interested and in deep need of learning, identifying and practicing authentic forgiveness.

Target Groups

Ideally, the invitation to learn and practice authentic forgiveness would be sent first to pastors, then to lay leaders, and finally to the entire congregation. While pastors and lay leaders would be earmarked as potential leaders for this ministry initiative, they would also benefit personally since they, too, will have the opportunity to learn and experience the transforming power of forgiveness and the joy of reconciliation in situations of unforgiveness in their own lives.

Conclusion

This chapter has provided a brief description of the plan which has inspired and motivated members of Jachin Church to understand and practice authentic forgiveness and to confront the tendency to trivialize it because of cultural influences. I pray that the same will inspire and motivate your church to learn, identify and practice authentic forgiveness as well as to experience the divine power of healing from our Heavenly Father in your own contexts.

6

Practice: Implementing the Plan in Your Church

The previous chapter set out a plan of action for promoting and practicing authentic forgiveness in your church. This chapter recommends a timeline for implementing this new ministry initiative for three groups of people: first, pastors; then, lay leaders; and subsequently, the entire congregation of your church. The implementation process begins with a pilot run, during which feedback from participants helps to continually refine the ministry plan. The chapter also discusses the physical and human resources required, how pastors and lay leaders will be selected, recruited, and trained to help others forgive, and the measures required to assess the effectiveness of the pilot run. Based on this assessment, adjustments will be made to the ministry initiative prior to the full launch.

The Pilot Run

The pilot run is a tool to help achieve the new ministry initiative of practicing authentic forgiveness in your church. It will first target pastors and subsequently lay leaders. The pilot run includes both teaching about authentic forgiveness and practicing it.

At the end of the pilot run, pastors and lay leaders who have embraced the process will be invited to become caring mentors and helpers for the small focus groups – facilitating, motivating, and guiding the people in these groups to deal with the hurt and conflict in their lives and to practice authentic forgiveness, whether as offenders or as victims. Once caring mentors and helpers are identified, recruited, and trained, this new ministry initiative can be launched for the entire congregation.

The effectiveness of the pilot run must be assessed on an ongoing basis, considering two aspects: cognitive learning and practice. The assessments will measure whether the participants have understood what authentic forgiveness is, whether they are able to confront its trivialization under cultural influence, and whether they are practicing it step by step.

Implementation Timeline

The implementation timeline outlines two phases of the pilot run and the full launch for the whole congregation, and assigns estimated completion dates to each. This timeline should be sensitive to your church calendar, so as not to disrupt existing ministries and programs – for instance, outreach events during the Christmas and Advent season, family events during Thanksgiving or New Year, and services related to Lent and Easter.

Pilot Run: Pastors (First Three Months)

The pastoral team should be the first to learn and then openly and transparently share their experiences of this new initiative. The learning and sharing can be done in the pastoral cell group. If there is none, a weekly two-hour small group can be set up for this purpose. Support from pastors is of paramount importance for both the pilot run and the full launch of this new ministry initiative.

During these first three months, there would be in-depth teaching to help the pastors understand what authentic forgiveness is and to motivate them to practice it. They will be encouraged to identify their own unaddressed hurts and go through the steps of practicing authentic forgiveness (as described in chapter 5) with close support and care from one another. If issues arise which require additional help, support may be sought from other pastors, counselors, clinical psychologists, or professors experienced in this area.

At the end of three months, thorough assessments should be carried out to evaluate the effectiveness of this new ministry initiative (details of this are discussed in the "Assessment" section below). Based on these assessments, the ministry plan may have to be revised. In the fifth month, caring mentors will be carefully selected and recruited from among the pastoral team to lead focus groups consisting of lay leaders (during the pilot run) and members of the entire congregation (during the full launch). The selection and recruitment of caring mentors is discussed in the "Development of Caring Mentors and Caring Helpers" section below.

Pilot Run: Core Lay Leaders (Fourth to Seventh Month)

The next phase in the pilot run is directed at the lay leaders of your church. Pastors are responsible for nourishing lay leaders, caring for them, discipling them, and giving them direction. Lay leaders, in turn, help pastors to nourish and care for church members. If lay leaders are to be equipped to guide other church members to properly perceive and practice forgiveness, it is vital that they themselves experience the blessing and transforming power of authentic forgiveness.

This phrase comprises two stages. The first includes five two-hour sessions aimed at teaching and helping lay leaders understand the theological and biblical foundations of authentic forgiveness, so that they can confront the tendency to trivialize it under cultural influences and practice it on their own. While some attention will be given to practice in the teaching session, the group will probably be too large to minister to those who have experienced deep pain and hurt. Such ministering will take place at the second stage, when lay leaders who want to deal with their hurt will be invited to participate in small focus groups. Each focus group will have one caring mentor, who will lead a maximum of six to eight lay leaders. As described in chapter 5, there will be worship, prayer, Holy Communion, and storytelling during the focus group sessions, in order to connect people with Jesus who embodies love, forgiveness, and communion. Participants will be reminded that they are grace-receivers, empowered by Jesus to be grace-releasers. The focus groups will meet biweekly for a minimum of five sessions. During these sessions, participants will be encouraged to walk through the concrete steps of authentic forgiveness as described in chapter 5.

In the eighth month, there should be quantitative and qualitative assessments to measure the effectiveness of the new ministry initiative (details are discussed in the "Assessment" section below) and the ministry plan may be revised and refined based on these assessments.

In the ninth month, caring helpers will be selected from among the core lay leaders and trained to help in the focus groups, alongside caring mentors, when the new ministry initiative is extended to the entire congregation.

Full Launch: Entire Congregation (Tenth to Fourteenth Month)

Implementation of the ministry initiative within the congregation can begin in the tenth month with a four-to-eight-week sermon series about authentic forgiveness. The sermon series should cover the story of Joseph and his brothers, and the parable of the prodigal son, along with the Scriptures highlighted in chapter 5. Suggested topics for the sermon series are given in appendix A.

Once the sermon series is complete, the entire congregation will have a basic understanding of the importance of practicing authentic forgiveness. As a follow-up, in the twelfth month, the church school or Sunday school can offer a course – similar to the teaching sessions conducted for core lay leaders – for church members who want explore more deeply the topic of authentic forgiveness. This course will go deeper into this topic than the four-to-eight-week sermon series because each service allows only about forty minutes of preaching and the diversity of backgrounds and needs within the church require sermons to be broadly outlined. In this smaller classroom setting, the course content can specifically target those in need in depth. Using the content of this book, pastors can teach during the course more thoroughly about what authentic forgiveness is and how to practice with steps, and can answer any questions raised by the church members.

Upon completion of the classroom teaching, participants who desire to practice forgiveness or repentance can join a small focus group, where sessions will be conducted along the same lines as for core lay leaders. Since church members may not be as spiritually mature as lay leaders, more care is needed in these groups. Therefore, each small focus group will have one caring mentor and one caring helper to listen to their stories, facilitate sharing and support of one another, motivate them to deal with their hurt and conflict, and encourage them either to forgive or to seek forgiveness and to work towards reconciling the broken relationship. During these sessions, the caring mentor will also carefully observe participants and decide if it is necessary to seek help from outside counselors.

Resources Required

Both material and human resources are required for this initiative. The primary material resources are the sermon notes and classroom teaching notes that will be used for the preaching and teaching portions of the new ministry initiative. Apart from this, resources required would include rooms of varying sizes to cater to large group learning as well as small focus groups, a sound system for worship and teaching, an audiovisual system such as a computer, projector, and screen, and the bread and cup for administering Holy Communion.

The human resources required are caring mentors and caring helpers who will guide and accompany those who choose to walk through the process of authentic forgiveness. It is necessary to have a pastor or a team of pastors dedicated to the pilot run, who will teach, guide, and accompany the participants, as well as train and supervise caring mentors and helpers. When required, outside help may be sought from pastors, counselors, clinical psychologists, or professors experienced in this area.

Development of Caring Mentors and Caring Helpers

Caring mentors are recruited from among the pastoral staff, while caring helpers are recruited from among lay leaders. Caring mentors will take the lead in the focus groups and caring helpers will assist. After the pilot run, those pastors and lay leaders who have embraced the authentic forgiveness taught and experienced in the class and in the focus groups could be invited to become caring mentors and caring helpers provided they satisfy the following key criteria: hospitality, availability, and maturity ("HAM").

Hospitality: since they must facilitate deep and open sharing by people of their hurts and pain, caring mentors have to be patient and caring, able to encourage participants to lay bare their hearts.

Availability: Those who become caring mentors will have to set aside time in order to take up this extra work. Forgiveness is difficult and complex, and it requires a lot of time and energy for the pastors to care for and guide those in need to seek healing, forgiveness, and reconciliation. Although caring helpers will serve much less intensively than caring mentors, they too must consider whether they can set aside the necessary time to assist in this task.

Maturity: Caring mentors need to be mature – not just spiritually but emotionally. Most pastors have already had training in pastoral care; but it is important that they be emotionally mature, stable, and healthy since they will have to listen to people's difficult and painful stories. The same holds true for caring helpers who assist the caring mentors. As mentors and helpers come alongside people to listen, to facilitate sharing, and to encourage them to take further steps – to let go and be healed by God, to reconnect with the offenders with forgiving hearts, to seek repentance by the offenders, to forgive and release the offenders, and to reconcile with one another – there could be many hiccups along the way. The journey towards reconciliation involves many complexities – such as internal struggles, false inner selves, lies, fear, false guilt, anger, shame, and grief. Caring mentors and caring helpers must be mature enough to guide, advise, and help people navigate this process.

If caring mentors and caring helpers themselves have struggled with and experienced authentic forgiveness, they are encouraged to share their stories. As discussed previously, storytelling is a healing narrative and one of the most powerful ways to invite and encourage others to practice authentic forgiveness and experience the divine gift of true reconciliation.

Measuring Effectiveness

Assessments to measure the effectiveness of the pilot run and the full launch will be carried out in each of the outreaches: to pastors, to lay leaders, and to the entire congregation. This will include both quantitative and qualitative measurement. In terms of quantitative measurement, the number of participants and their attendance will be recorded to assess if the sermon series and the course on authentic forgiveness were well received. With regard to qualitative measurement, since the new ministry initiative focuses on two aspects – cognitive learning and practice – attendees will be asked to evaluate the content of both these aspects using questionnaires. See appendix B for sample questions in the questionnaire. Based on the results of these assessments, adjustments should be made to the ministry plan to improve it.

Conclusion

This chapter has suggested a timeline for implementation of this new ministry initiative for three groups of people: pastors, lay leaders, and, finally, the entire congregation. It is also recommended that this ministry initiative be offered again – annually or biannually – for new pastors, new lay leaders, and new church members.

From my own experiences at Jachin Church and other institutes – both churches and seminaries – where I have shared this initiative, the responses have been amazingly positive. People have found both aspects – cognitive learning and practice – helpful; many have suggested a longer duration for these sessions; and almost everyone said that they would recommend this learning experience to others. Many have been healed and reconciled with others as they practiced authentic forgiveness. All this points to a deep need in people's hearts to experience God's gift of forgiveness and to embrace a new beginning as they are healed of hurt and pain.

As you prayerfully consider this initiative for your own church or institute, be prepared to tailor it to your own context and to continually refine it based on the responses to the ongoing assessments. May God guide you through this process so that his will would be done in your church.

7

Final Words: As We Have Been Forgiven, so Forgive

This book has addressed two key questions: What is true forgiveness? How can it be achieved? In life, no one can avoid conflict, sin, and evil, and these often cause hurt and brokenness. Forgiveness is a divine gift offered by God to overcome hurt, brokenness, bitterness, and hatred, in order to release people from their past, reopen the future, and empower them to risk further relationship.

Many are unwilling to live as forgiven and forgiving people, as people who seek to live in the light of God's reconciliation. They seek vengeance rather than forgiveness, domination and abuse rather than repentance and reconciliation, and repay violence with violence rather than with love.[1] The decision lies in the hands of each individual. Though it is countercultural to choose forgiveness and love of enemies over fighting and seeking revenge, disciples of Jesus are called to love and forgive as he did. Forgiveness is costly, but we desperately need it. Those who live under the shadow of deep pain and bitterness from the past can be healed and renewed by choosing forgiveness instead of unforgiveness.

This book seeks to motivate churches and individual Christians to understand and practice forgiveness that is theologically and biblically based. Such authentic forgiveness comprises two aspects: mutual recognition that repentance is genuine, and reconciliation of the broken relationship. Practicing

---

1. Jones, *Embodying Forgiveness*, 262.

authentic forgiveness brings transformation, both personally and communally that God intends.

Forgiveness, however, is understood and expressed differently in different cultures. Some forgive by overlooking, some by forgetting; some forgive to avoid conflict – without discussing in depth each party's responsibility – and some forgive to achieve self-healing without dealing with the broken relationship. Such deviations from biblically based forgiveness cannot fully renew people or empower them to break out of the cycle of brokenness and blind retaliation. The way that many Christians in Hong Kong practice forgiveness deviates from authentic forgiveness in various ways because their perception and practice of it are tainted by the cultural influences of Chinese tradition and Western individualism.

Chinese tradition pursues harmony as one of its core values. Harmony is generally regarded as something good; it becomes negative when people avoid discussing the details of the conflict and hurt in order to maintain harmony. Where injustice and deep hurt are involved, this usually results in decay of the relationship in the long run. Authentic forgiveness is not merely about harmony; it requires discussion of the issues in depth, genuine confession and repentance by one or both parties, and reconciliation.

Western individualistic culture upholds individual dignity and self-worth, and these are generally good things. But if individual self-care is promoted as the central value, then the needs of the individual become more important than the needs of the community. In individualistic cultures, forgiveness may turn from being an interpersonal bridge to become an intrapersonal process of self-healing that is unrelated to the community. Authentic forgiveness is not merely about an individual's own need and self-healing; it is a social transaction, restoring and reconciling broken relationships between parties.

During my twenty years of service as a deacon and pastor, I have made many mistakes in this area. There have been times I have misled people by asking them to forgive without taking sufficient care of their inner hurts, their need to pursue the offender's repentance, and their deep desire to mend the broken relationship with the offender. As a Chinese Christian in Hong Kong, who lived and studied for years in North America, I have been deeply influenced by both Chinese tradition and Western culture. Thus, I understand why many Christians in Hong Kong – and in countries with similar cultural backgrounds – sometimes hold an unbiblical view of forgiveness.

Authentic forgiveness is a divine means for humanity to break the cycle of bitterness, violence, and revenge. It seeks to put right past wrongs and release people on both sides from the consequences of these wrong actions.

To receive the full blessedness that God intends for humanity – both personally and communally – it is vital to confront the tendency to trivialize authentic forgiveness. Authentic forgiveness is a complex, time-consuming, and difficult process, but the results and rewards it yields are well worth the time, cost, and effort involved.

Andrew's Story

In conclusion, a story of authentic forgiveness is worthy of mention. Andrew is a fifty-five-year-old father and a disciple of Jesus. Andrew's birth was considered untimely because shortly thereafter his family almost went bankrupt and his father had an extramarital affair. Traditional Chinese are superstitious, and Andrew's parents believed that he had brought bad luck to their marriage and financial situation. As a result, Andrew was hated and neglected by both his parents during his childhood.

Andrew has two older siblings, and they were both abused physically and mentally. Approximately twenty-five years ago, when they could become independent, both of them left Hong Kong for good because they had suffered deep pain and hurt during their childhood and wanted to cut off the memories of their past.

Andrew's father did not have a stable job for many years. Their parents often quarreled, were drunk, and even fought each other from time to time. During Andrew's childhood, his father had several affairs and at times even brought his mistresses home. His mother had no one to turn to and left home a few times. Each time, Andrew and his siblings, who were in great fear and distress, begged their mother to come back home. In the end, she returned home, partially because of her need to take care of the children and partially because of the Chinese customary moral standard on marriage. At that time, no matter how bad a marriage's relationship became, it was customary that the couple sustained the marriage and the wholeness of the family, and avoided losing face in front of others. However, the parents' relationship was estranged.

Things began to change when Andrew came to know Jesus forty years ago. He hated his father, but God's love for and forgiveness toward Andrew has gradually transformed him. It took him six years to let go and be healed by God, and thus, he decided not to repay hatred with hatred but to forgive, though at that time he did not fully understand what biblical forgiveness involved. Andrew practiced love for his enemy. He also prayed for God's strength to love his parents and share the gospel with them as he believed God's healing on him should not merely be a unilateral act, but that there should be reconciliation among the family members. For the following fifteen years, he led all his family members to Christ and encouraged all of them to practice love towards each other and to reconcile.

He awaited genuine repentance and forgiveness to come. The relationship among family members has gradually improved in the following ten years. God's word has been shaping them and the Holy Spirit has been transforming them. Andrew's parents began to soften and change their attitude toward each other and toward Andrew.

Fifteen years ago, his mother amazingly confessed and apologized to Andrew's wife for the wrongful acts done to Andrew in his childhood. As it is very difficult for traditional Chinese to apologize to their children, she did not talk to Andrew directly, but she talked to Andrew's wife. Ten years ago, his father, who never cared explicitly for Andrew's growth and never remembered his birthday, unexpectedly sent him a birthday card to show his care. Trust between them began to germinate.

Regarding forgiveness and reconciliation, a major breakthrough occurred approximately five year ago after they were encouraged, through teaching and storytelling at Jachin Church, to face the misdeeds seriously. Andrew's mother, in tears, asked for prayer fervently for God's strength to give her a forgiving heart to forgive her husband due to his irresponsibility to run the family and the mistresses he had. She began to confront Andrew's father. His father became serious in his faith in Christ and proclaimed in front of pastors that he would repent from his past misdeeds and follow Jesus.

At the sixtieth wedding anniversary of his parents, an amazing thing happened. Andrew arranged a feast and invited thirty close relatives to celebrate it. One of Andrew's siblings came back to Hong Kong to attend the feast.

To everyone's surprise, Andrew's father said that he wanted to pray. Andrew was nervous as his father had never prayed in public. His father suddenly began to cry and pray loudly. He thanked God for his wife, and confessed that for so many years in the past, he had done a lot of wrongful acts against his wife and the family. He said he was an irresponsible person and yet his wife still supported him and his children still loved him. He also thanked God for the close relatives who supported them in their times of financial difficulties.

Chinese seldom openly confess their failures in public and deliberately lose face. It was incredible that his father confessed and apologized openly to both those he hurt and to God in his prayer. All the hearts of those who were there were melted, and almost all cried with joy, love, forgiveness, and acceptance in response to the sincere apology. Then Andrew's parents hugged each other and reopened a new future as authentic forgiveness had occurred gradually throughout the years.

Andrew said that since his father has genuinely followed Jesus, he has transformed to be a more caring father and husband. There may still be many difficulties as they seek to reconstruct their relationships within the family. But the way the parents dealt with hurts openly and sincerely in front of one another and in front of God, which is countercultural, has blessed all the family members with healing, trust, mutual respect, and reconciliation.

Authentic forgiveness with genuine repentance and reconciliation has occurred in this deep, personal, and enduring pain. It took decades for Andrew's family to forgive and reconcile. Authentic forgiveness is a long and complex process, but it is one of the most valuable gifts God offers to humanity. It is hoped that this book leads to more stories like Andrew's, as God has infinite gifts of deep healing for those who are willing to pursue authentic forgiveness.

Appendix A

Sermon Series Topics and Scriptures

Inevitability of conflict, sin, and hurt: *Adam and Eve, Cain and Abel, Joseph and his brothers, David and Bathsheba, Prodigal Son*

Reconciliation with one another before worshiping God: *Matthew 5:23–24*

Guidance by the Holy Spirit: *John 14:16–26; 15:26–27; 16:12–14; 20:21–23*

Retelling our stories to God and to godly people: *Psalms 36; 42; 43; 69; 139; Romans 12:15; Ephesians 4:16*

Releasing anger without sin: *Ephesians 4:26–27*

Forgiveness is not an option: *Matthew 6:12, 14–15*

Forgiveness is a complex process rather than a single act: *Joseph and his brothers*

Repentance is a must for authentic forgiveness: *Joseph and his brothers, Prodigal son with lost sheep and lost coin*

Repentance brings real change and reconciliation: *Joseph and his brothers*

Confession and remorse: *Joseph and his brothers, Prodigal son*

Restitution: *Leviticus 6:1–7*

Renewal: *Joseph and his brothers*

Discovery of similarity: *1 Kings 19:4; Matthew 6:12–15; Matthew 18:23–35; John 8:2–11*

Resume valuing and loving others: *Genesis 1:26–27; 1 John 4:20*

Forgiving habit (forgiving without keeping count): *Luke 17:3–4; Matthew 18:21–22*

Love your enemy even if the offender does not repent: *Matthew 5:38–45; Luke 6:27–28*

When justice demands confrontation: *Matthew 18:15–17*

Appendix B

Authentic Forgiveness Questionnaire: Sample Questions

Please circle. On a scale of 1 to 5, 1 means least satisfied, 5 means most satisfied

		Least satisfied				Most satisfied
1.	The content is consistent with the topic of authentic forgiveness	1	2	3	4	5
2.	The content provides sufficient theological and biblical foundation	1	2	3	4	5
3.	The content can be practiced in daily life	1	2	3	4	5
4.	The content has helped you to grow spiritually when dealing with hurt, conflict, and forgiveness	1	2	3	4	5
5.	The teacher has sufficient knowledge of the topic	1	2	3	4	5
6.	The teacher has adequate presentation skills to clearly present the content and to arouse your interest in learning and practicing	1	2	3	4	5
7.	The teacher has inspired and motivated you to reflect on what authentic forgiveness is and to practice it	1	2	3	4	5
8.	The class includes sufficient time for questions to be asked and addressed	1	2	3	4	5
9.	The class clearly and comprehensively explains what authentic forgiveness is	1	2	3	4	5
10.	The class explains well the trivialization of authentic forgiveness under the cultural influence of Chinese tradition and Western individualistic culture and motivates you to confront such trivialization	1	2	3	4	5

11. The class clearly explains the steps to be taken to practice authentic forgiveness	1	2	3	4	5
12. The class encourages you to embody authentic forgiveness in your daily life	1	2	3	4	5
13. If you have practiced the steps for authentic forgiveness in the past few weeks – the steps are helpful	1	2	3	4	5
14. If you have joined a small focus group – the small focus group is helpful	1	2	3	4	5

Would you recommend others to attend this class the next time the church offers it? Yes/No

Reason:

Suggest ways for the church to improve this initiative:

If you have joined a small focus group, please answer the following questions:

1. Has your hurt and pain been addressed? If YES, how satisfactorily?

2. Have you been helped to be healed, to repent/ reconcile with one another?
   a. If yes, how? Please describe your hurt and how you have experienced authentic forgiveness with healing, repentance and reconciliation.
   b. If no, why not?

3. How has the experience of authentic forgiveness impacted your life? How has it impacted your relationship with God and with others?

4. How can the church improve the small focus group?

5. Do you need further follow-up by the church? If so, please give your name and contact details, and also describe briefly your hurt and pain and the way you hope the church can help.

Other:

We may wish to use your story (without mentioning your name) to encourage others to learn about and practice authentic forgiveness. Do you give permission to use your story? (indicate YES or NO)

Bibliography

Augsburger, David W. *Conflict Mediation across Cultures*. Louisville, KY: Westminster John Knox, 1992.

———. *Dissident Discipleship: A Spirituality of Self-Surrender, Love of God and Love of Neighbor*. Grand Rapids, MI: Brazos Press, 2006.

———. *Helping People Forgive*. Louisville, KY: Westminster John Knox, 1996.

———. *The New Freedom of Forgiveness*. Chicago, IL: Moody, 2000.

———. *Pastoral Counseling across Cultures*. Belleville, MI: Westminster Press, 1986.

Barth, Karl. *Church Dogmatics* IV/1, trans. G. W. Bromiley. Edinburgh: Clark, 1956.

Blackaby, Richard. *Spiritual Leadership: Moving People on to God's Agenda*. Nashville: Broadman & Holman, 2011.

Bock, D. L. *Luke: The NIV Application Commentary*. Grand Rapids, MI: Zondervan, 1996.

Bonhoeffer, Dietrich. *The Cost of Discipleship*. Translated by R. H. Fuller. New York: Macmillan, 1963.

———. *Life Together*. San Francisco: HarperCollins, 1965.

Caproasia. "2016 Stock Exchange Market Capitalization." Accessed 21 April 2017. http://www.caproasia.com/2017/01/27/2016-stock-exchange-market-capitalization/.

Cheuk, Fei Man and Check Yim Cheng [文灼非和鄭赤琰。] 《中國關係學》 [*The Studies of Chinese Relationship*]. Hong Kong: Hong Kong Chinese University Asia Research Centre, 1996.

Dostoevsky, Fyodor. *The Brothers Karamazov*. Translated by R. Pevear and L. Volokhonsky. San Francisco, CA: North Point Press, 1990.

Finley, James. *Christian Meditation: Experiencing the Presence of God, a Guide to Contemplation*. San Francisco, CA: HarperCollins, 2004.

Fitch, David. *The Great Giveaway: Reclaiming the Mission of the Church from Big Business, Parachurch Organizations, Psychotherapy, Consumer Capitalism, and Other Modern Maladies*. Grand Rapids, MI: Baker Books, 2005.

Foster, Richard. *Celebration of Discipline: The Path to Spiritual Growth*. San Francisco, CA: Harper & Row, 1978.

Gane, R. *Leviticus: The NIV Application Commentary*. Grand Rapids, MI: Zondervan, 2004.

Guder, Darrell L. "The Church as Missional Community." In *The Community of the Word: Toward an Evangelical Ecclesiology*, edited by Mark Husbands and Daniel J. Treier, 114–128. Downers Grove, IL: InterVarsity Press, 2005.

Hart, Thomas. *Hidden Springs: The Spiritual Dimension of Therapy*. Minneapolis, MN: Fortress, 2002.

Hong Kong Exchange. "Market Statistics 2016." Accessed 21 April 2017. https://www.hkex.com.hk/eng/newsconsul/hkexnews/2016/Documents/1612202news.pdf.

Jones, L. Gregory. *Embodying Forgiveness: A Theological Analysis*. Grand Rapids, MI: Eerdmans, 1995.

Kerr, Michael and Murray Bowen. *Family Evaluation*. New York, NY: Norton, 1988.

May, Gerald. *The Dark Night of the Soul: A Psychiatrist Explores the Connection between Darkness and Spiritual Growth*. San Francisco, CA: HarperCollins, 2004.

———. *Will and Spirit*. San Francisco, CA: HarperCollins, 1982.

McClendon, James W. *Ethics: Systematic Theology, Volume I*. Nashville, TN: Abingdon, 1986.

McNeal, Reggie. *A Work of Heart: Understanding How God Shapes Spiritual Leaders*. San Francisco, CA: Jossey-Bass, 2011.

Milbank, John. *Theology and Social Theory*. Oxford: Blackwell, 1990.

Moltmann, Jurgen. *The Spirit of Life: A Universal Affirmation*. Translated by Margaret Kohl. Minneapolis, MN: Fortress, 1992.

———. *The Trinity and the Kingdom: The Doctrine of God*. Translated by Margaret Kohl. San Francisco, CA: HarperCollins, 1981.

Moore, Thomas. *The Care of the Soul*. San Francisco, CA: HarperCollins, 1992.

Nouwen, Henri J. M. *The Return of the Prodigal Son: A Story of Homecoming*. New York, NY: Doubleday, 1994.

Ogne, Steve, and Tim Roehl. *TransforMissional Coaching*. Nashville, TN: Broadman & Holman, 2008.

Patton, John. *Is Human Forgiveness Possible?* Nashville, TN: Abingdon, 1985.

Peace, Richard. *Meditative Prayer: Entering God's Presence*. Colorado Springs, CO: NavPress, 1998.

Peters, Ted. *Sin: Radical Evil in Soul and Society*. Grand Rapids, MI: Eerdmans, 1994.

Russell, Jeffrey Burton. *The Prince of Darkness: Radical Evil and the Power of God in History*. Ithaca, NY: Cornell University Press, 1988.

Schilling, S. Paul. *God and Human Anguish*. Nashville, TN: Abingdon, 1977.

Smedes, Lewis B. *Forgive and Forget: Healing the Hurts We Don't Deserve*. San Francisco, CA: HarperCollins, 2007.

Snodgrass, K. *Ephesians: The NIV Application Commentary*. Grand Rapids, MI: Zondervan, 1996.

Soelle, Dorothy. *Suffering*. Minneapolis, MN: Augsburg Fortress, 1975.

Suchocki, Marjorie Hewitt. *The Fall to Violence: Original Sin in Relational Theology*. New York, NY: Continuum, 1995.

Surin, Kenneth. *Theology and the Problem of Evil*. Oxford: Blackwell, 1986.

Tao Lai, Julia Po-Wah. "Reconstruction of Traditional Values for Culturally Sensitive Practice." In *Marriage, Divorce, and Remarriage,* edited by Katherine P. H. Young and Anita Y. L. Fok, 267–289. Hong Kong: Hong Kong University Press, May 2005.

Tillich, Paul. *Love, Power, and Justice. Ontological Analyses and Ethnical Applications*. London: Oxford University Press, 1954.

Tyler, Anne. *Saint Maybe*. Westminster, MD: Ballantine, 1992.

Volf, Miroslav. *Exclusion and Embrace: A Theological Exploration of Identity, Otherness, and Reconciliation.* Nashville, TN: Abingdon, 1996.

Walton, J. H. *Genesis: The NIV Application Commentary.* Grand Rapids, MI: Zondervan, 2001.

Whitney, Barry L. *What Are They Saying about Good and Evil.* Mahwah, NJ: Paulist, 1985.

Wiesenthal, Simon. *The Sunflower on the Possibilities and Limits of Forgiveness.* New York, NY: Schocken Books, 1998.

Willard, Dallas. *The Divine Conspiracy.* New York, NY: HarperCollins, 1998.

 **Langham**
PARTNERSHIP

Langham Literature and its imprints are a ministry of Langham Partnership.

Langham Partnership is a global fellowship working in pursuit of the vision God entrusted to its founder John Stott –

to facilitate the growth of the church in maturity and Christ-likeness through raising the standards of biblical preaching and teaching.

Our vision is to see churches in the majority world equipped for mission and growing to maturity in Christ through the ministry of pastors and leaders who believe, teach and live by the Word of God.

Our mission is to strengthen the ministry of the Word of God through:
- nurturing national movements for biblical preaching
- fostering the creation and distribution of evangelical literature
- enhancing evangelical theological education

especially in countries where churches are under-resourced.

Our ministry

Langham Preaching partners with national leaders to nurture indigenous biblical preaching movements for pastors and lay preachers all around the world. With the support of a team of trainers from many countries, a multi-level programme of seminars provides practical training, and is followed by a programme for training local facilitators. Local preachers' groups and national and regional networks ensure continuity and ongoing development, seeking to build vigorous movements committed to Bible exposition.

Langham Literature provides majority world preachers, scholars and seminary libraries with evangelical books and electronic resources through publishing and distribution, grants and discounts. The programme also fosters the creation of indigenous evangelical books in many languages, through writer's grants, strengthening local evangelical publishing houses, and investment in major regional literature projects, such as one volume Bible commentaries like *The Africa Bible Commentary* and *The South Asia Bible Commentary*.

Langham Scholars provides financial support for evangelical doctoral students from the majority world so that, when they return home, they may train pastors and other Christian leaders with sound, biblical and theological teaching. This programme equips those who equip others. Langham Scholars also works in partnership with majority world seminaries in strengthening evangelical theological education. A growing number of Langham Scholars study in high quality doctoral programmes in the majority world itself. As well as teaching the next generation of pastors, graduated Langham Scholars exercise significant influence through their writing and leadership.

To learn more about Langham Partnership and the work we do visit **langham.org**

Lightning Source UK Ltd.
Milton Keynes UK
UKHW021237210120
357347UK00007B/379